VINEGAR

The Complete Guide to Making Your Own

VINEGAR

The Complete Guide to Making Your Own

Dr Caroline Gilmartin

THE CROWOOD PRESS

The *Tacuinum sanitatis* is an eleventh-century illustrated handbook written by Ibn Butlan of Baghdad, in which he presents the elements needed for a healthy happy life. He particularly recommends vinegar for problems with bile and the gums. A woman stands on a ladder filling a pitcher with vinegar while a man watches. WIKIMEDIA COMMONS

CONTENTS

Preface   6

1 Introduction   7
2 A Potted Vinegar History   10
3 The Fermentation Process   20
4 Reasons to Make your Own Vinegar   30
5 General Equipment Requirements and Cleaning   33
6 How to Make Your Own Vinegar   43
7 Optimising Acetification   58
8 Monitoring Acetification   67
9 Troubleshooting the Vinegar-Making Process   76
10 Vinegar Recipes Using Ready-Made Alcohols   85
11 Preparing Alcohol Bases for your Vinegars   89
12 Alcohol Base Recipes   112
13 All-in-One   125
14 Scrap Vinegars   130
15 Vinegar Food and Flavour   135
16 Using Your Home-Made Vinegars   144
17 Vinegar for Health – Is It a Superfood?   156
18 Vinegars in the Home   160

Vinegar for Fun   164
A Summary of the Dos and Don'ts of Vinegar Making   166
Appendix: Producing Vinegar for Business   167
References   168
Glossary   171
List of Suppliers   172
Further Reading   173
Index   174
Acknowledgements   176

PREFACE

What do most of us know about vinegar? Not a lot, it seems. Though we might have five or six types in the cupboard, our ubiquitous and ancient condiment is largely taken for granted. While we instinctively reach for it to add the acidity our palates seek, few of us know the back story – complex microbial interactions and 10,000 years of history!

Home-made and shop vinegar are a world apart.

Alcohol and vinegar are inextricably linked: without the former you can't have the latter. The process is as ancient as life on earth, an intricate dance between plants, yeasts and bacteria that will happen whether we intervene or not, but which we have learned over the millennia to control.

Handmade vinegars bear little resemblance to the mass-produced versions on supermarket shelves: they will be complex, delicious and unique.

This is a pastime that cannot be rushed because nature will not allow this to happen, but we can coax it along with a little understanding of the process. Vinegar making can be as simple or as complicated as you like; there are various starting points, also parameters, such as acidity, that you can measure or ignore. Vinegar can be produced with minimal scientific knowledge and specialist equipment, or it can be monitored closely for more precise results. This book will explain the science and history behind the vinegar, talk you through the most successful methods for home and small-scale craft production, and give you some delicious recipes to try.

While I have endeavoured to keep to the vernacular, there is a glossary at the back for jargon busting – and please don't be put off by the maths: why not embrace the challenge? Fear not, because although it is helpful for measurements, vinegar making can be done without it.

CHAPTER 1

INTRODUCTION

WHAT IS VINEGAR?

I asked 380 adults (via an Instagram poll) if they knew where vinegar came from. Respondents could answer a) yes, b) I've a vague idea, or c) I've not a clue. The results can be seen in the chart.

Bearing in mind that a large proportion of those who replied work in the fields of either food or health, and as only 12 per cent knew the answer, let's start at the very beginning! And as a starting point, here is a simple definition:

Vinegar is the result of a natural transformative process that is essentially a tale of two microbes: yeasts that turn sugar into alcohol, and acetic acid bacteria (AAB) that subsequently turn the alcohol into vinegar. Without alcohol, you can't make vinegar.

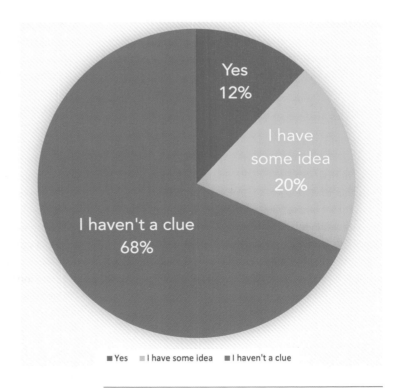

The breakdown of Instagram poll responses to the question 'do you know how vinegar is made?'.

Yes ■ I have some idea ■ I haven't a clue

We can expand this for some more detail:

> Vinegar is a solution that contains 4–9 per cent acetic acid in water. It is produced in a two-step fermentation process. Firstly, yeasts break down sugar in fruit juice or grain mash to produce alcohol. Secondly, AAB convert the alcohol to vinegar in the presence of oxygen. It contains a range of bioactive components including organic acids, amino acids and phenolics, and has culinary, medical and household uses.

Etymology

Working backwards, our English version of the word comes from the French *vin aigre*, which means sour wine. In turn, this was derived from the Latin *vinum acer*, meaning the same. When malt vinegar first became popular in the fifteenth century it was known as *alegar*, as opposed to vinegar, as it was produced from ale, not wine, although this term has now died out (almost – *see* page 85).

ACETIC ACID

Acetic acid is an organic chemical compound (the scientific meaning of organic is 'carbon containing'). It also has another name that you might come across: ethanoic acid. It is the component that gives vinegar its characteristic sour taste and pungent smell. The written formula and the molecular structure can be seen in the illustration.

Pure and undiluted it is called 'glacial' acetic acid because of the ice-like crystals that form at just below room temperature. In its glacial form it is highly corrosive, and its vapour is irritating to the eyes, nose, throat and respiratory system. Even at the low concentration found in vinegar, acetic acid can cause coughing, burning and streaming eyes!

Acetic acid can be produced in two distinct ways: in a laboratory using chemical reagents, or biologically with microbes.

Chemical Production of Acetic Acid

Vinegar existed thousands of years before anyone had heard of acetic acid, which wasn't identified as its

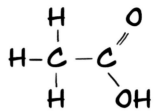

$$CH_3COOH$$

The molecular structure of acetic acid, where the C stands for carbon, the H for hydrogen, and the O for oxygen.

major component until the eighth century, by Persian alchemist Jabir ibn Hayyan (*see* box). During the Renaissance, German alchemists extracted pure acetic acid from the pigment copper acetate, and as early as 1648 an industrial process had been developed to isolate it by burning wood in a vacuum.

Until the late 1700s, it was assumed that the acetic acid found in vinegar was different to the pure glacial form; however, a scientist called Pierre Adet realised that it was the same thing, but dilution in water changed the characteristics.

Nowadays, industrial chemical processes such as methanol carbonylation and aldehyde oxidation are used for rapid acetic acid production on a grand scale, with a global market worth a massive USD 20.6 billion.[1] This is a consequence of its versatility: it is used in the production of plastic bottles, wood glue, synthetic fabrics, chemical compounds, descaling and cleaning products, and as an acidity regulator in food with the additive code E260.[2] It can also be safe for human consumption when diluted (*see* below, page 158).

The biological production of acetic acid is the focus for the rest of the book – the natural result of the action of yeasts and AAB on suitable carbohydrate substrates, resulting in vinegar. We'll be looking in greater detail at the microbes and processes involved in Chapter 2.

What Vinegar is Not

When you go to your local chippy and they ask you if you'd like salt and vinegar on your chips, did you

JABIR IBN HAYYAN

Jabir Ibn Hayyan developed methods for distillation, and discovered citric acid (the sour component of citrus fruits) and tartaric acid (from wine lees), as well as hydrochloric and nitric acids. In those days, the dream of the alchemist was to be able to create pure gold – however, his combination of hydrochloric and nitric acids was able to dissolve gold, but the making of it evaded him. He was a prolific discoverer of processes we still use today, including distillation and the use of manganese dioxide in glass manufacturing to prevent the green tinge produced by iron. He also noted that upon boiling wine, a flammable vapour was released, paving the way for the later discovery of ethanol, the other essential part of our vinegar story, by another Iranian, Abu Baki al Razi, a few years later.

know that this is not technically vinegar? It is usually a diluted solution of industrially produced acetic acid mixed with caramel as a colouring agent, and as such is devoid of the complexity of flavour and nutritional compounds that result from natural fermentation processes. This product must be labelled NBC – non-brewed condiment, to distinguish it from vinegar. This was the result of legal action pursued by vinegar manufacturers in 1950, which went all the way to the House of Lords,[3] as they attempted to protect their businesses from this cheap and non-authentic competition.[4] The result was that anything described as vinegar must be the product of the double fermentation process (alcoholic followed by acetic), performed by microbes.

Fish and chips and non-brewed condiment! This cannot be called vinegar as it is made from industrial (food safe!) acetic acid coloured with caramel. DryWhite is the UK's best-selling brand. DRYWHITE

CHAPTER 2

A POTTED VINEGAR HISTORY

It would be remiss of me to gloss over vinegar's fascinating history, as the processes we will be using have developed over thousands of years – so here is a whistlestop tour. There are two tales here: first, how the relationship between yeasts and AAB arose; and then the human perspective – how vinegar became so integral to our lives that we completely take it for granted.

MICROBES AND VINEGAR

Vinegar microbes have a long history of symbiotic association; you can see this in action as a mother of vinegar forms on the surface of a freshly made batch. This is a type of biofilm formed by a mass of microbes growing together within a cellulose matrix, similar in principle to a kombucha SCOBY or kefir grains. These are fascinating manifestations; bacteria and yeasts themselves can't be seen without a microscope, yet they can produce these tangible and very visible entities.

Prokaryotes, including anaerobic bacteria, developed about 3.5 billion years ago. The evolution of *Cyanobacteria*, which could photosynthesise and produce oxygen, led gradually to the presence of aerobic bacteria, such as AAB, around 3.1 billion years ago (according to a new genetic analysis of dozens of families of microbes).[5]

Symbiotic relationships exist in other fermented foods: kombucha, water kefir, milk kefir and mother of vinegar are all examples of biofilms.

More complex, single-cellular yeasts (eukaryotes) developed about 2.7 billion years ago through endosymbiosis, whereupon smaller microbes became incorporated into larger ones. After the appearance of fruiting bodies of plants, about 125 million years ago, yeasts developed the ability to rapidly convert simple sugars into ethanol. This gave them a selective advantage because ethanol is toxic to many microbes, but yeasts can tolerate quite high levels. Over time, yeast ethanol metabolism and AAB use of alcohol as an energy source became aligned. Today both AAB and yeasts are ubiquitous in nature, on and in plant surfaces, soil and air.

HUMANS AND VINEGAR

While much is known about the origins of alcohol production, it is harder to pinpoint exactly when vinegar 'began'. At first people didn't know how to stop wine from turning into vinegar, and in many instances there might not have been much difference between the two – it's fair to say that ancient wines would have been rather challenging for our palates.

Researchers at the University of Pennsylvania discovered 9,000-year-old Neolithic jars at Jiahu (Henan province, China) in which were detected traces of the earliest known alcoholic beverage. It appears to have been a delicious sounding mixture of wild grapes, hawthorn berries, rice and honey. Remnants of early wine manufacture are also scattered throughout the Middle East, but it's not clear who, if anyone, can claim the rights to the 'invention' of vinegar.

The earliest known wines: a delicious-sounding mixture of wild grapes, hawthorn berries, rice and honey.

Vinegar Over the Ages
The Babylonians
The first written record of vinegar has been identified as dating from Babylonian times. By 3000BC, Babylonian civilisation was well established, and the deciphering of cuneiform symbols inscribed upon clay tablets tells us

Alcohol traces were found in fragments of jars from the neolithic period. ADOBE STOCK that they were great innovators, with winemaking an important industry.

Although vines were grown, dates grew better, so date beer/wine was the mainstay. The Babylonians knew that vinegar was able to prevent the deterioration of foodstuffs, and it was extensively used in preservation (more so than as a seasoning). Preservation was an activity that occupied much of our forebears' time, as the seasonality of produce meant that storage was of paramount importance. As soured date-beer vinegar was abundant, it was more economical than using salt (*see* page 129 to find out how to make your own date or raisin vinegar). As viticulture spread throughout the Mediterranean, so did the presence of vinegar.

The Romans

In Roman times, diluted vinegar known as 'posca' was the drink of slaves and soldiers. It was safer than drinking plain water as the effect of vinegar in terms of water purification was known, even if the agents of disease were not – and one supposes that it made for a sober workforce and army too!

It was common in Roman households to have a vinegar-containing dish called an acetabulum on the table at mealtimes. As we know, the Romans were great feasters, and between courses it was usual to dip bread into it and consume this as a palate cleanser. This is

interesting, given what we have recently learned about the ability of vinegar to help regulate glucose levels (*see* page 156).

Lucius Columella, who lived during the first century, in his text *De Re Rustica* (*Farming Topics*), presents the very first written recipes for the use of vinegar both in the kitchen and as a medicine (*see* page 126 for Columella's fig vinegar recipe, which you can try yourself).

Rather unfortunately for them, the Romans also developed sapa, a delicacy of sweetened, boiled grape syrup. This they prepared by boiling fermented grape must in lead pots. Acetic acid in the must reacted with

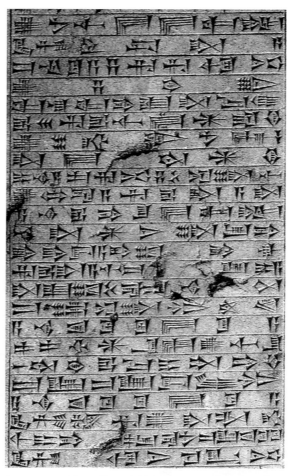

An example of cuneiform tablets that were deciphered to reveal the first written mention of vinegar – sadly not the exact ones. Wikimedia commons

An acetabulum was found at every Roman feast (Museum August Kestner, Hannover). Marcus Cyron

the pots, causing high concentrations of lead acetate in the sapa, and consequently, lead poisoning among the aristocracy.

The Romans even had a verb for the act of boiling down grape must into a syrup: *defrutare*. It is likely that this tradition of boiling must eventually developed into the production of balsamic vinegar (*see* page 138).

The Ancient Greeks

The ancient Greeks had their own, far more beneficial version of a vinegar beverage. Oxymels were comprised of water, vinegar, honey and herbs. The physician Hippocrates, also known as 'the father of modern medicine', prescribed oxymels as salves for wounds and sores, and to be imbibed for the treatment of respiratory diseases. The Greek scholar Theophrastus (371–287BC[6]) described how vinegar reacted with metals to make mineral pigments such as white lead and verdigris from copper, for artistic use.

Ancient Islamic Civilisation

By AD700, the use of vinegar in ancient Islamic civilisation was also well established. The prophet Mohammed said: 'Allah has put blessings in vinegar, for truly it was the seasoning used by the prophets before me.' Although alcohol is considered *haram*, or forbidden according to the laws of Islam, vinegar is *halal*, or permitted.

This put a different perspective upon its production, because while the alcoholic starting material, most likely date beer, would have been without value, the opposite was true of vinegar. A one-step process was used for production, whereby fruit juice was given optimal conditions to turn to vinegar via simultaneous development of alcohol and acetic acid. (*See* page 125 for how to set up all-in-one vinegars.)

Europe

By the end of the fourteenth century, vinegar was firmly on the map as a genuine industry, centred in Orléans, France. This had grown hand-in-hand with the development of the French wine industry: the aristocracy had developed a taste for the fine wines of the Bordeaux, Loire and Rhône regions, most of which were barrelled and then transferred to barges that travelled up the River Loire to Orléans, the nearest major river port to Paris, for distribution via local wine merchants.[7]

Once unloaded, the wine would be inspected by a team of *piquers-jureurs*, or quality control inspectors. Anything failing to make the grade was sold to local vinegar and mustard makers: vinegar was in high demand as a food preservative. With Orléans as a hub for over-oxidised fine wines, these became the bases for similarly fine vinegar. The process used was to lie aerated barrels on their sides to age for several months; this became known as the 'Orléans method', and is still used today. Orléans vinegar maintained its reputation until the French Revolution, whereafter industrialisation, and the use of cheap distilled spirits and global competition, caused its demise. From 300 producers pre-Revolution, today just one of the original vinaigriers, Maison Martin Pouret, survives.

A paintbox with mineral pigments; vinegar was reacted with metals to make them. DADEROT

Boats transported wine barrels along the Loire to Orléans where they were checked before leaving for Paris – taxes were payable, and no one wanted to pay taxes for undrinkable wine. ALAIN DARLES

The range of vinegars available from Martin Pouret, the last traditional vinegar maker in Orléans. MARTIN POURET

Across the pond in the UK, in 1845 there were 65 London-based vinegar makers, using products including raisins, beer, gin and wood as bases for vinegar production. These days, big names including Sarson's, Aspall and Manor Vinegar produce much of the regular malt and distilled fare, although there has been an upsurge in the production of raw apple cider vinegar (ACV) with the mother from both large and smaller producers.

After the Industrial Revolution to the Present Day
Since the Industrial Revolution vinegar production has, like everything else, been automated, but traditional methods and principles are still very much in evidence. Of the four processes described below, three are still in use in industry today, and we will be adapting these to make our own vinegar later (*see* section on page 44).

The Orléans Process (Surface Method)

The Orléans process is still used today for traditional vinegars such as balsamic and Jerez. Wooden barrels are laid on their sides to increase the surface area, with covered orifices for aeration to provide oxygen for the AAB. A covering of cellulose forms, and as the oxygen moves across this barrier, a concentration gradient is set up, with continuous diffusion of finished vinegar downwards. This can be tapped off at intervals, and fresh wine added. This is done using an in-situ long funnel that can add the alcohol to the bottom of vessel without disturbing the mother of vinegar. The process takes time – between months and many years, leading to excellent flavour development. Operating on a continuous culture basis, long slow evaporation and ageing, coupled with enrichment of successive barrels, leads to complex, flavoursome vinegars.

A series of barrels showing the Orléans process. Barrels are laid on their sides for increased surface area. On each you can see the air holes and level indicator. MARTIN POURET

THE ORLEANS PROCESS

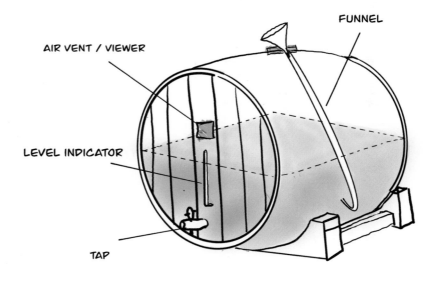

AIR VENT / VIEWER

FUNNEL

LEVEL INDICATOR

TAP

A diagram showing the set-up of an Orléans vinegar barrel.

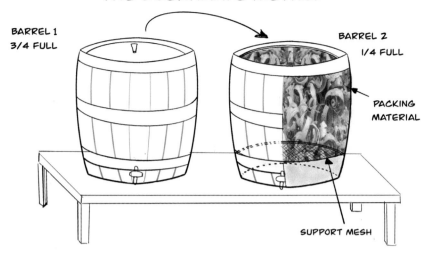

THE BOERHAAVE METHOD

BARREL 1
3/4 FULL

BARREL 2
1/4 FULL

PACKING MATERIAL

SUPPORT MESH

A diagram showing the Boerhaave process.

The Boerhaave and Trickly Methods (Quick Process Acetifiers)

The first major upgrade to the Orléans method was the work of Dutch scientist Herman Boerhaave (1668–1738).[8] The principles of his method are increased aeration and surface area for optimal AAB activity. Wooden sticks or old vines were placed in each of two barrels, with plenty of room for liquid to be

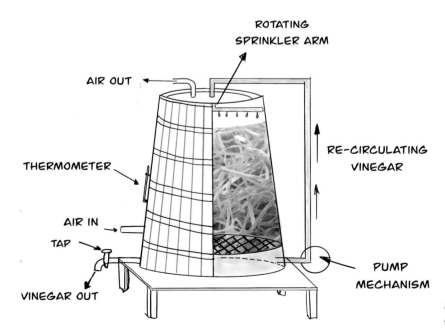

'TRICKLY' GENERATOR

ROTATING SPRINKLER ARM

AIR OUT

THERMOMETER

RE-CIRCULATING VINEGAR

AIR IN

TAP

PUMP MECHANISM

VINEGAR OUT

A diagram showing the set-up for the trickling acetifier.

poured between. Something would be put across the sticks to keep them in place. The first barrel would be three-quarters filled with wine; the second, a quarter filled. Twice daily the wine in the fuller cask would be emptied into an emptier one, leaving one quarter behind. The constant tipping to and fro of the wine would oxygenate it, the sticks providing a much larger surface area for AAB to grow on than just the surface of still wine. The wine left in the bottom of the cask would prevent the sticks drying out. This would speed up the process immensely, and wine vinegar could be made within a month. In Chapter 7 we will see how to make a small-scale Boerhaave system – this is my favourite way to make vinegar at home.

German chemist Karl Schüzenbach (1793–1869) further mechanised the Boerhaave process. Instead of two barrels, he filled just one with wine to the level of a false bottom. This was recirculated through a pipe with a rotating sprinkler attachment, so it would trickle down over the packing, thus continuously exposing the wine to AAB, and the bacteria to the air. The heat produced from the reaction could increase the efficiency to produce vinegar of 10 per cent acidity within three or four days. Packing materials such as these are still commonly used in industrial systems – for example the Welsh larchwood wool used by Sarson's Malt Vinegar Company to this very day.

The Continuous Submerged Method (Acetator)

Submerged fermentation is the pinnacle of modern industrial production. High-grade vinegar can be

Modern acetators are not to be confused with acetifiers! These highly regulated machines include cooling columns, aeration, stirring, and strict control of every imaginable parameter to make vinegar very quickly! ADOBE STOCK

produced in just 24 hours when specially selected strains of AAB are stirred with pumped pure oxygen, rather than just being left to grow on the surface.

Oxygen is fed directly into a tank containing a source of alcohol and microbes, which is stirred with an impeller. Nutrient levels, temperature, aeration, circulation rate and the ethanol:acetic acid ratio must be closely controlled. If aeration is too high, evaporation occurs, potentially lowering the yield. If there is a problem with the oxygen supply for as little as a minute, mass death of microbes can occur and a complete restart is needed. This method has been further adapted and refined by Heinrich Fring, founder of the company that today supplies acetators to the vinegar industry worldwide.

VINEGAR MYTHS AND LEGENDS

Vinegar is at the root of many famous tales; the following are some of the most interesting, if not the most credible!

The Inventor of Vinegar?

There is an ancient Chinese tale of a wine maker, Heita son of Du Kang (approximately 2000BC), who apparently invented vinegar. He thought it wasteful to discard wine lees, so he stored some in a jar. When he reopened it sometime later, the aroma of sweetness and sourness filled his nostrils and he couldn't help but taste it… Thus, vinegar as a condiment was born, and perhaps even helped to form the basis of Chinese medicine.[9]

Cleopatra's Pearls

In his *Natural History,* Pliny the Elder relates that Cleopatra, the last of the Egyptian queens, owned the two largest pearls of all time. They were worth millions of sesterces. To demonstrate ultimate superiority in extravagance over her lover, the Roman leader Marc Antony, she bet that she could spend ten million sesterces on a single meal. He accepted the wager; she fed him a sumptuous meal, which was delicious but clearly not that valuable, and he laughed, thinking he'd won. She explained that the best was yet to come. For the next course, servants brought a dish containing

Heita, son of Du Kang. Did he invent vinegar? Perhaps – in any case it's an interesting theory.

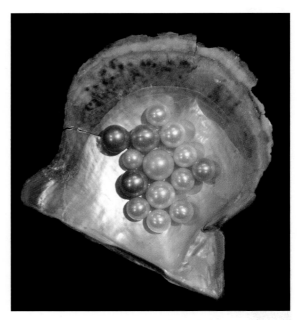

Cleopatra – a queen not to be reckoned with. HANNES GROBE/AW1

vinegar, into which she plunged one of the pearls. When it was dissolved, she swallowed it, thus winning the bet.

This had been dismissed as fiction; recently, however, classicist Prudence Jones of Montclair State University in New Jersey conducted an experiment to show that a supermarket strength vinegar (5 per cent w/v acetic acid) takes 24 to 36 hours to dissolve a solid pearl weighing about a gram. When the pearl is crushed and the vinegar warmed, the reaction time is reduced to about ten minutes. Pearls are composed of calcium carbonate, which is soluble in acetic acid. It didn't happen quite as quickly as Pliny's report would have us believe, but it really did work! It is certainly possible that Cleopatra, who was known to have carried out toxicological experiments, might have pre-softened the pearl to speed things up.[10]

Hannibal and the Impassable Pass

Hannibal, the great Carthaginian general, undertook his famous trek across the Alps from Spain to conquer Rome. According to the Roman historian Livy (Titus Livius 59BC–AD17), Hannibal's army used the technique

A Bronze Age example of how rocks were hollowed, in the Austrian Alps. ANDREAS G. HEISS

of fire-setting to clear rocks that were obstructing their path. Fires were set against a rockface to heat the stone, which was then doused with vinegar, the thermal shock causing the stone to fracture. Limestone rocks can be dissolved by the acetic acid in vinegar, but it would require a lot of it; in this case it is most likely that the physical reaction was more effective than the chemical one. Perhaps the soldiers were carrying vinegar for drinking and used this instead of water.

The Crucifixion

Vinegar has several mentions in the bible, but the best known occurs in the gospel descriptions of the crucifixion (Matthew 27:48, Mark 15:36, and John 19:29). Soldiers offered Jesus vinegar on a stick soaked in a hyssop sponge. This was extremely likely to have been posca, the diluted 'sour wine' drunk by soldiers, which would probably have been nearby for their refreshment. This interpretation rather changes the perspective of the offer from one of cruelty to one of kindness.[11]

Vinegar and Jealousy

The Chinese word for eating vinegar is 吃醋, which is made up of 吃, the verb 'to eat', and 醋, the word for 'vinegar'. However, as a phrase this doesn't simply mean 'eat vinegar' – it means 'to be jealous'. During the Tang Dynasty (AD618–907) there was a prime minister called Fang Xuanling. He was a good man, reputedly very much in awe of his wife, Lady Lu. As a reward for his hard work, the emperor gave him two concubines – but Fang was so scared of his wife's reaction that he sent them back to the palace.

The emperor was very upset at the rejection of his lovely gift, and called the couple to the palace for a conference. He gave Lady Lu two options: either to allow her husband to take the two ladies home, or to drink a glass of poison. With no hesitation, Lady Lu grabbed the glass of poison and downed it in one. Fang Xuanling was beside himself, but soon realised that the whole assembly was laughing, because it was not in fact poison, but vinegar, and the emperor had been testing Lady Lu! One assumes that after this, she was able to go home with just her husband, leaving the concubines behind.[12]

CHAPTER 3

THE FERMENTATION PROCESS

To recap, vinegar is a product of two separate microbial fermentations: alcoholic fermentation by yeasts, then acetic fermentation by AAB. The stages can occur either sequentially or concurrently, depending on which method you choose (more on this later, *see* page 44). First, let's look at the microbes and the biological reactions in some more detail.

Microbes, which are so called because of their microscopic nature, can be thought of as tiny factories. Each makes all the components it needs to create a whole new microbe whilst producing a myriad of other things, including alcohols, acids, vitamins and enzymes. AAB and yeasts are both microbes, but they are fundamentally different creatures.

YEASTS AND THEIR FUNCTION

Yeasts are members of the fungus kingdom. Even though they still only exist as single cells, they are, like us, eukaryotes, with a nucleus of DNA contained in a membrane. They also contain organelles – tiny sub-factories where protein manufacture and energy production occur. Yeasts are an important part of everyday life, and essential for processes including beer-, wine- and breadmaking as well as biofuel production – and, of course, Marmite.

There are about 1,500 identified species, but the one that is most important in this context is *Saccharomyces cerevisiae*. A study examining yeasts on grapes used for

JUICE   YEAST   WINE   WINE   VINEGAR MOTHER & MICROBES   TIME   OXYGEN   VINEGAR

An overview of how vinegar is made: sugars in the juice are converted by yeast into alcohol. Then alcohol is converted to vinegar by acetic acid bacteria (AAB).

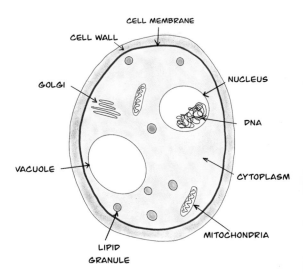

The structure of a yeast cell, showing the nucleus that contains the DNA; the organelles, including the mitochondria, which generate energy; and the golgi apparatus that packages proteins.

making a natural wine found nine species present at the beginning of fermentation (such as *Pichia, Candida, Zygosaccharomyces, Hanseniaspora*), but by the end of fermentation only *S. cerevisiae* remained. It almost always dominates because it is extremely efficient at

Louis Pasteur (1822–1895) – one of the greatest microbiologists of the Victorian age – invented pasteurisation, discovered acetic acid bacteria as spoilage agents in wine, ascribed fermentation to yeasts, set up a microbiology institute… PAUL NADAR

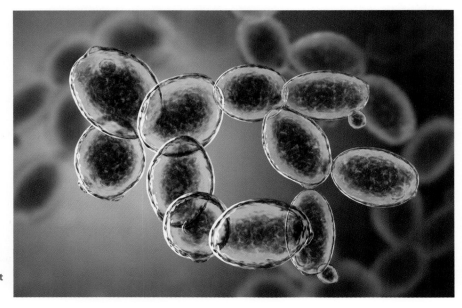

Electron micrograph of reproducing yeast cells – new ones form by budding, and here small buds are forming that will grow in size until they split off. ADOBE STOCK

metabolising sugar. In fact the name *Saccharomyces* can be translated as sugar fungus, with the *cerevisiae* part meaning 'of beer' in Latin. There are many different strains with various characteristics, making them suitable for brewing or baking, for example – we'll look at this in detail later (*see* page 104).

In 1857 Louis Pasteur formally identified yeasts as living creatures responsible for making alcohol in wine; hitherto a chemical process was thought to be responsible, and yeast cells incidental.

Yeasts are facultative anaerobes, which means they can produce energy through different pathways, depending on whether oxygen is present (respiration) or absent (alcoholic fermentation). They produce nine times more energy through aerobic respiration.[13] Despite this, if sugar is in plentiful supply, some yeasts will still make alcohol even in the presence of oxygen, a phenomenon called the Crabtree effect. This seems very inefficient and the reasons aren't clear – maybe they do it for fun!

When yeast is added to a must, it enters a lag phase, during which it makes sterols (lipids) that are essential for membrane reinforcement; yeasts with strong membranes are more resistant to alcohol and more efficient at fermenting and replicating. Sterol building requires oxygen. The microbes then enter a growth phase: under optimal conditions, they multiply exponentially, doubling every 100 minutes or so, and can live for about 25 cycles before dying, and sinking to the bottom of the jar.

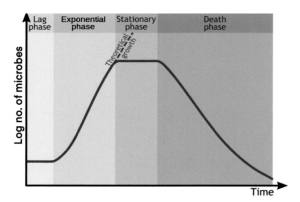

Yeast growth dynamics: lag phase, during which sterols are produced, leading to exponential growth phase, followed by stationary phase, where nutrient availability and growth are stabilising, then the death phase where nutrient depletion occurs. MICHAEL KOMORNICZAK

How Yeasts Produce Alcohol

Yeast can use a variety of sugars to make alcohol. Glucose and fructose can be used straight away, but sucrose and maltose need to be cleaved into simple sugars via the enzyme invertase. Glucose and fructose are transported into the yeast by hexose transporters – membrane proteins that act like gates in the cell wall.

Then begins a complex series of events, and yeasts will either ferment or respire depending on their environment. This reaction occurs quite happily at room temperature. It also generates heat that isn't

The invertase reaction, which splits sucrose into glucose and fructose (and maltose into glucose).

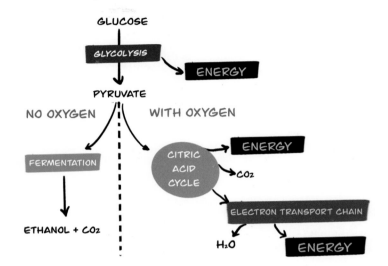

GLUCOSE

GLYCOLYSIS → ENERGY

PYRUVATE

NO OXYGEN ⟵ ⟶ WITH OXYGEN

FERMENTATION

CITRIC ACID CYCLE → ENERGY
→ CO_2

ELECTRON TRANSPORT CHAIN

ETHANOL + CO_2

H_2O → ENERGY

Fermentation pathway in yeast, through which alcohol is produced.

noticeable on a small scale, but in industrial settings, cooling can be required.

ACETIC ACID BACTERIA (AAB)

AAB are prokaryotes, the simplest of creatures – a level down from eukaryotes, we could say, with just the most basic cellular machinery. They are a large family of microbes, four types of which are of particular interest to us, because they are directly involved in the manufacture of vinegar and kombucha. These are *Acetobacter*, *Gluconobacter* and the succinctly named *Komagataeibacter* and *Gluconacetobacter*. While they are diverse enough to have different names, they all oxidise ethanol to acetic acid.

AAB are rod-shaped or oval, occurring singly, in pairs or in chains. They do not form spores, and often have flagella, which are structures like tadpole tails that can help them swim in liquids. They are aerobes, requiring oxygen for growth and reproduction, and thrive in acidic environments, between pH3 and 6.5. Most prefer temperatures between 26 and 30°C, though they can make vinegar at lower temperatures more slowly.

Other characteristics include, for some, the production of copious quantities of cellulose, which

we see as vinegar mother, or kombucha SCOBY. This cellulose matrix serves as a support framework to enable the microbes to grow at the air-liquid interface, and also helps to protect them from harsh environmental conditions.

Louis Pasteur can also claim the credit for establishing the importance of AAB in fermentation. In 1856 he was commissioned by a manufacturer of beetroot wine to determine why the product kept spoiling. When he examined the microbes in the wine he found oval, plump yeast cells in normal beet juice, but in spoiled batches there were also smaller oval-shaped microbes. He identified them

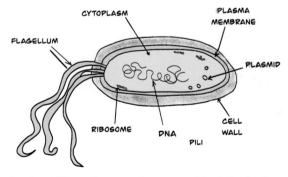

CYTOPLASM · PLASMA MEMBRANE · FLAGELLUM · PLASMID · RIBOSOME · DNA · CELL WALL · PILI

Acetic acid bacteria are prokaryotes, with minimal cell machinery.

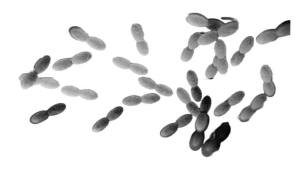

An electron micrograph of *Acetobacter aceti* in pairs (coloured). ADOBE STOCK

Celluose production is common in AAB, but not all strains are producers.

as *Acetobacter* sp., the agents of wine spoilage and vinegar production.

AAB are ubiquitous in nature, even in soil where they promote plant growth through nitrogen fixing.

They are used commercially for the bioproduction of cellulose; bacterial cellulose is strong, and much purer than the plant-based version, which is usually entangled with lignin. Due to its excellent water-holding capacity, high tensile strength and biocompatibility, it has therapeutic applications including for burn, wound and ulcer repair.

Curiously, many strains of AAB are not that tolerant to the acetic acid they produce and can struggle to survive in strong vinegar – the same goes for high concentrations of alcohol, and above 10 per cent they die off. Acetic acid bacteria have a far slower doubling time than yeasts – up to twelve hours at room temperature, compared with about 90 minutes for brewer's yeast. This explains why vinegar can take so long to form, and why so much effort has been expended in optimising the process (*see* page 58).

$$C_6H_{12}O_6 \longrightarrow 2C_2H_5OH + 2CO_2$$

GLUCOSE	ETHANOL	CARBON DIOXIDE
1 MOLE	2 MOLES	2 MOLES
180 G	92 G	88 G
1 KG	506 G	494 G
250 G	126.5 G.	123.5 G
19.8 G	10 G (1%)	

This chemical equation will underpin much of the optimisation of the alcohol-making process. One mole of glucose makes two moles of ethanol and two moles of CO_2. One mole of glucose weighs 180g. One mole of ethanol weighs 46g. One mole of CO_2 weighs 44g. Calculations show that 1kg of glucose can produce about 500g of both ethanol and carbon dioxide. If you put that kilo of sugar into 4ltr of water, you can produce about 130g/ltr ethanol, which equates to 13 per cent. This is where the idea that 250g/ltr sugar is the required quantity for making wine. The equation also shows that for every 1 per cent of alcohol produced, 19.23g of sugar is required.

HOW AAB USE ETHANOL TO PRODUCE ACETIC ACID

In the second stage of the process, AAB convert alcohol into acetic acid. Oxygen (air) is required, and there are two separate steps. In the cytoplasm are thousands of different enzymes. Two of these, alcohol dehydrogenase and aldehyde dehydrogenase, are involved in breaking down alcohol – this can be seen in the illustration.

Firstly, alcohol is oxidised to acetaldehyde and water; then with more oxygen, acetaldehyde is oxidised to acetic acid. This reaction produces heat, and although it can occur slowly well below room temperature, the microbes prefer a warmer 24–28°C. Some acetic acid will also react with the remaining alcohol to make ethyl acetate, emitting strong solvently odours – this is a reversible reaction, and is a sign that fermentation is underway but not yet complete.

Some of the resulting acetic acid is used to generate energy for the cell, the rest is exported by a transporter mechanism in the cell wall, to the external medium, thus making vinegar. Both actions reduce the intracellular acetic acid concentration, which if it rose too high, would kill the bacterium.[14]

In the absence of alcohol, AAB can oxidise sugars for energy – and if they're really starving, they can use their own acetic acid that they've made, oxidising it to carbon dioxide and water; we will talk about how to avoid this reaction destroying all your hard work later (*see* page 66).

The Yield of the Reaction

The theoretical yield of the vinegar-making process is as follows: one quantity of sugar can be fermented into almost equal quantities of alcohol and CO_2. This quantity of alcohol can then be converted into an equal quantity of vinegar. However, in real life the process isn't this efficient. Working backwards, to end up with vinegar at 5 per cent acetic acid, about 7 per cent alcohol is recommended. In turn, to make a 7 per cent alcohol mash, approximately 14 per cent sugar is needed at the start. The bottom line is, you need enough sugar to make enough alcohol convert to vinegar.

MOTHER OF VINEGAR

Making vinegar is all about the 'mother': this is a biofilm, a conglomeration of AAB and the cellulose they produce. It can grow as a shiny layer at the air-liquid interface, or exist as a murky swirl at the bottom of a

OXIDATION OF ETHANOL TO ACETIC ACID

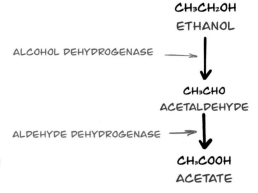

ETHANOL
CH_3CH_2OH

ALCOHOL DEHYDROGENASE →

CH_3CHO
ACETALDEHYDE

ALDEHYDE DEHYDROGENASE →

CH_3COOH
ACETATE

The two steps in the conversion of alcohol to acetic acid. The reaction also requires a co-factor called purroloquinoline (PQQ) and calcium.

bottle. It even has its own botanical name: *Mycoderma aceti*.

The mother exists to help AAB congregate at the liquid-air interface, so that they can have good access to oxygen. It also protects them from stressful growth conditions, including high alcohol and acetic acid concentrations, and may also reduce the rate of evaporation from the alcohol base during slow processes.

Overall, the presence of a visible mother is desirable – not just for the reasons given above, but because it's a clear indication that something is happening. However, not all types of *Acetobacter* produce cellulose, but they can still make vinegar.

Both liquid and cellulose mothers are valid – both can make new batches of vinegar.

The top centimetre of this fermentation box is semi-solid cellulose mother.

In fact, in industrial production, it helps if they don't produce much, or the machines can get clogged up. I have made wild, all-in-one batches of apple cider vinegar with no visible sign of cellulose mother at all.

Therefore liquid vinegar from an actively, well stirred batch is just as valid as an inherited cellulose disc – in fact I think it is preferable, as the microbes can then be distributed throughout a new batch, making the most of dissolved oxygen and then developing a fresh cellulose disc if you are lucky.

Why Use a Vinegar Starter?

This is not necessary for all-in-one wild fermentations, given the ubiquitous nature of AAB, though that's not to say you can't add some to help things along. Eventually colonisation may occur in non-wild batches too if you're prepared to wait.

But there are good reasons to inoculate with a starter: it will speed up fermentation, decreasing losses due to evaporation over time and increasing the yield. Adding vinegar to the system can also protect against the growth of unwanted organisms such as surface yeasts, or moulds that can occasionally take hold.

How to Get a Vinegar Mother

Grow Your Own from Scratch

In wild fermentations, a visible vinegar mother may grow, although it can take up to six weeks of no intervention or stirring once the solids have been strained out. Vinegar may still form without any sign of cellulose mother. As already mentioned, the cellulose part is not essential, and the liquid can still be used to seed future batches.

Buy a Starter

Unlike sachets of commercial yeast, cultures of *Acetobacter* are hard to buy in small quantities, and extremely costly to buy in large amounts! You can purchase a ready-grown vinegar mother online quite easily – but if you choose this route, do ensure that the vinegar mother is fresh. They usually arrive as discs in a little liquid – add both and be prepared for the disc to fall to the bottom. I would stir the new batch well and remove the disc after 72 hours – before a new mother forms.

Mother of vinegar in a bag.

If you did have access to pure, commercially available *Acetobacter* species for vinegar production, you would need to ensure that you chose a strain with:

- High alcohol tolerance
- High acetic acid tolerance
- Wide temperature range
- Low nutrient requirements

Make a Starter Using Raw ACV

Another option is using raw apple cider vinegar, which is widely available and contains the mother we need. You can see it as a cloudy swirl in the bottom of the bottle as opposed to a floating disc of cellulose. After bottling and consequent oxygen exclusion, the microbes will be fairly dormant, but they can be resuscitated to make fresh vinegar.

The instructions for setting up a reliable starter culture are on page 45 – hopefully you will set up yours and will soon be ready to use it to inoculate.

Note: Unless the bottle uses the words 'raw' or 'live' or 'contains mother of vinegar', you will not be able to use the starter for this purpose – it will have been pasteurised and won't contain any live microbes.

In order to be able to start a new batch of vinegar, the starter must be live or raw or contain the mother.

Vinegar Mother Growth

Although mother of vinegar forms at the interface of liquid and air, it is not naturally buoyant and if the fermentation vessel is disturbed it will fall to the bottom. If you are impatient and constantly poking at it, it will be hard to make a robust cellulose mat. If a mother falls to the bottom of the vessel it should be removed, as it will absorb oxygen, thus removing it from the system, which can end up slowing down fermentation. Don't worry, as a new mother will begin to form at the surface.

For strong surface growth of vinegar mother, the following two additions can help:

Sugar
Sugar provides an energy source for AAB to make the cellulose from – as little as 1 per cent (10g/l) will suffice. If there is no sugar in the alcohol base there will be

There is a huge mass of sunken cellulose lurking at the bottom of this jar. It should be removed promptly.

MOTHER OF VINEGAR VERSUS KOMBUCHA SCOBY

At first sight vinegar mothers and SCOBYs might seem similar – both are cellulose discs, floating atop semi-clear brews – but there are visible and biological differences:

- SCOBYs float, vinegar mothers only do so until disturbed, and fall very easily. This is because SCOBYs contain a lot more CO_2 gas within their structure, which gives them buoyancy. If poked they will nearly always resurface.
- SCOBYs are more robust than vinegar mothers, which are more like a soft-set jelly with a much higher water content – they almost melt.
- SCOBYs contain, like vinegar mothers, a range of microbes, but these are not as tolerant to either high alcohol or acetic acid concentrations, so the amount of either alcohol or vinegar produced is limited – usually to about 2.5 per cent acetic acid. Large quantities of gluconic and glucuronic acid are also present in kombucha.

The differences between vinegar mothers and SCOBYs are subtle yet significant.

poor or non-existent mother growth; you can choose between adding a teaspoon of sugar to help this along, or adding fruit juice instead of water if diluting a high alcohol-content source (*see* page 55).

Nutrients

Micronutrients are often present in complex home-made fruit wines, but are absent from distilled and highly processed alcohols. A pinch of yeast nutrient (1g/l) or a splash of beer or fruit juice can help acetic fermentation along.

How to Maintain a Vinegar Mother Starter

Vinegar cultures can exist indefinitely, just like sourdough starters, with some families maintaining them for generations. The following are some pointers to keeping yours going:

- The more active the starter, the more quickly it will be able to start another batch of vinegar. A continuous culture in a vessel with a tap that can be topped up fortnightly with fresh alcohol is ideal (*see* page 83).
- Another way is to remove some vinegar from a newly started batch, early in the process, a couple of weeks in. At this point, microbes will be in prime condition, before they start to struggle with high levels of acetic acid, and will easily be able to seed a new batch.
- Bottled, newly completed vinegar and cellulose mothers remain active for about a fortnight in storage at cool room temperature, but gradually fall into dormancy. If you are not going to need a starter imminently, it is better to freeze it: the microbes recover more quickly if frozen in a healthy state than if you try to get them going from dormancy. If using a glass bottle, do make sure you leave at least 20 per cent room for the expansion that will occur during freezing, and label clearly.
- Alternatively, you can store some live vinegar in a jar either with or without the cellulose, with a lid and a little headroom (a couple of inches). Every couple of weeks you can tip off 10 per cent of the volume of the vinegar and replace with 50/50 wine and water, beer, or 1:3 vodka and fruit juice. This will provide enough alcohol and nutrition to prevent complete dormancy of the microbes so they can reactivate more rapidly.

Freezing is a surprisingly effective way of ensuring that a vinegar mother remains fit and healthy.

Storing mothers in a jar means that they are on hand to share – but if you give them away, remember to give away some liquid starter too.

CHAPTER 4

REASONS TO MAKE YOUR OWN VINEGAR

With about 30 different types of vinegar available in any large supermarket, you might be wondering what could possibly drive a person to make their own. If you are on the fence, hopefully one of the following reasons will resonate.

FERMENTING FOR FUN

For anyone slightly curious about the invisible microbial world around them, this is the perfect pastime. It would be hard not to be amazed when you spot the faintest signs of a vinegar mother forming on the surface of a batch, or to witness the fermentation process in full swing with a froth of bubbles in primary fermentation.

It is not particularly labour intensive, it results in something useful, it can be undertaken with little expense, and gives you something to look forward to – it is akin to giving your future self a present! It can be as easy or as complicated as you like – either making your own alcohol, or using ready-made juice, or existing alcohol bases. If you choose, there is all sorts of kit available, but also no shortage of ways to improvise at home. There is a requirement for patience, though, which can be an issue for some of us.

With just a few methods up your sleeve, virtually every possible combination of fruit, vegetable or source

The selection of vinegars in a standard UK supermarket.

of alcohol can be turned into vinegar. There are few rules to follow and it is quite hard to go wrong, so it is one of the easiest ways in the kitchen to start to engage your inner biotechnologist. Celebrate your successes and your failures, and the uniqueness of every batch.

SUSTAINABILITY

Vinegar production is an enormous global industry. If you want to step away from big business and all that it stands for, here is the ideal opportunity: vinegar production requires little or no energy, you can re-use glassware, and can make the most of locally available seasonal produce, using gluts and preventing waste. Actually it's even more profound than that, as vinegar from gluts and waste can in turn be used to preserve future gluts, preventing even more waste!

You have the opportunity to know the provenance of everything you are using, and if you choose your starting material wisely, it can be extremely cost effective. For example, a litre of commercially available raw, organic ACV can cost upwards of £11 – but free apples, using an existing starter, can be vinegarised for just a few pence per litre (and then only if you need to add a little sugar).

TRADITION AND RECONNECTION

Vinegar making is an art that humans have developed over the past 7,000 years, out of a need to preserve precious foodstuffs and to deal with seasonal gluts. However, nowadays we live in relative luxury – we don't even need to know how to make basic foods ourselves because it's all done for us. But in the back of my mind, I always worry along the lines of 'what will we do when the revolution comes?' The pandemic panic-buying fiasco and the besieged Ukranians in Mariupol have really made me think about this. Complacency can be dangerous, and it's important to keep traditions alive for history, understanding, and even potentially for our survival.

Microbes are involved in every aspect of our being – from our own gut microbiota to nitrogen fixing in the roots of the crops we consume, even in the biotechnology industry to make food additives and vitamin supplements. The fermentation process will reconnect you with our invisible super heroes, as they bubble away making alcohol or creating thick mats of cellulose and vinegar, and with the produce you are using, too.

FLAVOUR AND CREATIVITY

Home-made vinegars can provide more complexity and depth of flavour than most commonly available and affordable vinegars, as well as providing nuance to your cooking. They contain a variety of flavours and aromas, arising from alcohols, organic acids, esters, aldehydes, ketones, terpenes and volatile phenols, which arise from the base starting products, the microbes involved and also any ageing you might do. Some vinegars are more complex than others – balsamic vinegar, for example, can contain almost 100 different volatile organic compounds.[15]

These beautiful apples were given to me by friends in Cornwall – I made 4ltr of ACV!

It's hard to find unusual vinegar flavours in the shop.

Also it's much easier to make your own unusual vinegars than to buy them – for example carrot, beetroot, tomato and persimmon vinegars are all delicious but hard to come by, bar via a few artisan producers. In terms of creativity, the scope of what you can use to make vinegar, and/or to flavour vinegar, is virtually infinite, and this book barely touches the sides. But I hope you'll be able to take the principles and apply them using whatever appeals and is available.

HEALTH

Home-made vinegars can contain a whole range of bioactive components both from the fruits, vegetables

A shot a day keeps the doctor away?

and grains you've used to make them, and the work of the microbes. The use of vinegar as an adjunct to health is gaining traction (*see* page 156), and there is mounting evidence to suggest that having your own on hand to dilute for daily consumption could be a good move.

FOOD SAFETY AND VINEGAR MAKING

Due to vinegar's potent antimicrobial power, there are few risks involved in its production. However, if you were to use, for example, a jacket potato that was wrapped in silver foil and stashed for several weeks to make 'moonshine', as did American prisoners some years ago, you could be in trouble. The potato contained spores of *Clostridium botulinum* that were able to germinate in the anaerobic foil environment, making a nasty toxin that once created cannot be destroyed.[16] Don't

do this, check and amend the pH when making vegetable wines, and you are unlikely to have any food safety issues with your vinegar making.

However, don't forget the importance of using your senses to guide you. We are dealing with natural systems here, and with the best will in the world, no troubleshooting guide is going to be able to predict exactly what you might find. If your fermentation, at either alcoholic or acetic stages, looks different from what is described or shown, take a moment to work through some options, consulting the troubleshooting sections (*see* page 76).

CHAPTER 5

GENERAL EQUIPMENT REQUIREMENTS AND CLEANING

When it comes to vinegar making it is often easy to repurpose existing items. That said, there are several things that will make your life easier. The following are general items that will be useful throughout the vinegar-making process; more specific items are discussed in context in their relevant sections.

A note on batch size: how much vinegar you are making will influence the equipment you use. In this book we will mostly be focusing on making volumes between 1 and 5ltr, though you can, of course, scale up with multiple vessels. Cleanliness matters: contamination can cause unnecessary batch losses, so we will also discuss keeping things clean.

GENERAL EQUIPMENT

Containers

Containers made from food-safe glass, ceramic (check that the gaskets are acid safe), plastic, or appropriate food-grade stainless steel are all suitable for use throughout both alcoholic and acetic fermentation.

Do not use metal containers unless they are food-grade stainless steel (marked 304 or 316), as the alcohol and vinegar could react with the metal (let us recall the ancient Romans' love of posca that was fermented in lead containers, *see* page 12). Beautiful glass vessels made for decorative purposes may also contain lead.

For both alcoholic and acetic fermentation stages, you will need two vessels – one to ferment in, and another to rack into, to separate out the sediment.

Food-Grade Plastic Buckets

Food-grade plastic buckets from brewing shops are a good choice for making up to 10ltr of vinegar from start to finish, and can also be used for both alcoholic and acetic stages. They are available in multiple sizes to suit your needs. Bear in mind that cheaper versions do not have strong handles, which can be problematic if you need to move them. For alcoholic fermentation you can

Plastic buckets can often be repurposed from bulk-buy food items.

add an airlock, and then after racking (*see* Filtering off the Lees, page 107) you can cover with a cloth for surface-based acetic fermentation. You can also add a plastic tap about 8cm from the bottom to make racking easier.

Smaller Glass Vessels

For smaller quantities of alcohol and/or vinegar, more esoteric unusual flavours or experimenting, a 1 or 2ltr glass mason jar is a good choice, especially if you have an air-lock valve assembly. A jar with a wide aperture could also be used for the acetic fermentation stage, the wider the better.

Demijohns

While not strictly necessary for the alcohol process, 5 or 8ltr demijohns remain a popular choice, especially for secondary fermentation. Using glass has advantages: you can see how the lees are settling, and demijohns are quite hard to contaminate with their narrow necks. The disadvantages are that they are heavy, breakable, and hard to clean (but *see* a trick on page 41). Because of their narrow openings, demijohns aren't suitable for acetic fermentation – the airflow isn't sufficient, and if your vinegar grows a mother across the top, you won't ever be able to get it out of such a narrow-necked bottle!

A demijohn is ideal for large-scale secondary fermentation.

All these glass vessels will be useful for primary fermentation or all-in-one vinegars.

Drinks Dispensers

A 3, 5 or 8ltr glass or plastic drinks dispenser with a tap can be an excellent all-round choice. The aperture is wider, allowing for better air exchange, so these vessels can be used for all stages of production, from making bases to surface or continuous methods (*see* page 83). The transparency means that you can see what's going on, and with the tap it is easy to separate the fruit or vegetable wines from the lees, by draining into one of the aforementioned plastic buckets until the level of the tap is reached, then emptying out the lees and returning the fermented wine to the vessel (you can use the lees to make your own yeast nutrient, *see* page 108).

A tap dispenser is affordable and practical – but keep it away from bright sunlight to avoid hot spots in warm weather.

A vinaigrier is aesthetically pleasing and keeps the light out, giving an air of mystery!

Vinaigriers

If you are looking for something more aesthetically pleasing than a plastic bucket, there are some lovely options for surface fermentation: a vinaigrier is a ceramic pot with a tap dispenser and a lid that sits on top but is not airtight. Vinaigriers are of French origin, as the name suggests.

Wooden Barrels

If you are planning to age your vinegar before using it, there are real advantages to using wood. As with wine, there is the potential to add depth of flavour and even other bioactive components from the wood itself.[17] Barrels exist in sizes from 1 to about 225ltr. For best results, a previously aged barrel is your best choice; new barrels can have a strong resinous smell that doesn't always work with vinegar. Most people recommend soaking them for about six months in red wine first. However, if you've bought one especially for the purpose you can always take your chances.

If you are lucky enough to come by a wooden barrel, your vinegar is likely to be more nutrient rich.

The cheesecloth in the middle has too big a weave. Paper towel or finely woven cotton are best.

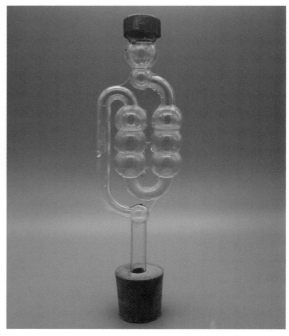

An S air lock allows CO_2 to escape without allowing oxygen or contaminants in. Simply fill the U-bend with distilled vinegar or alcohol.

Suitable Covers for Vessels

When you've located the perfect vessel for your batch, it will need a breathable cover. When making vinegar or carrying out a primary alcoholic fermentation when making your own bases, a degree of air flow is required. However, it is also necessary to keep out fungal spores that could cause mould and, even more importantly, fruit flies. The best solutions are closely woven cotton fabrics (not loose-weave cheesecloth as they can work their way through multiple layers), or a piece of good quality kitchen towel or a coffee filter. You can also use a plate or other solid, but not air-tight, fitting to minimise evaporation as long as you remove it daily. Save those large rubber bands that the postman drops on the path – they'll be invaluable for securing fabric to a 5ltr bucket.

Airlocks for Fermentation

There are several different forms of airlock, but the principle is the same: they are a way of excluding oxygen and contaminants from your brew, while maintaining an anaerobic (oxygen-free) environment, and allowing carbon dioxide from yeast fermentation to escape, thus eliminating the risk of explosion from gas build-up.

S-shape or 'bubbler' airlocks are commonly used with demijohns or in fermentation buckets, with a bung that fits exactly into the hole. While you can use water just to form a barrier between the air and the ferment, through which the carbon dioxide can percolate, I recommend using vodka or distilled vinegar as a basic antimicrobial approach.

For smaller quantities, simpler valves can fit mason jars, such as the Mason-top or Sterilock valves illustrated.

Failing that, you can make your own airlock, using a sturdy food-safe sandwich bag filled with water and alcohol, folded over the top of the vessel and sealed with a rubber band. This will keep air out, and rise and fall as CO_2 is produced, which will seep out around the rubber band. For show you can also use a rubber glove!

A Siphon Hose

A siphon hose is a useful way of transferring liquid from one receptacle to another, especially for larger volumes. Siphon hoses often come with a racking cane pump attached to set the pressure-driven motion in action, or a hand-operated squeezing mechanism.

Two commercially available one-way airlocks, allowing CO_2 to escape, and one home-made version using a plastic bag weighted with water.

Showy, impressive, but also effective!

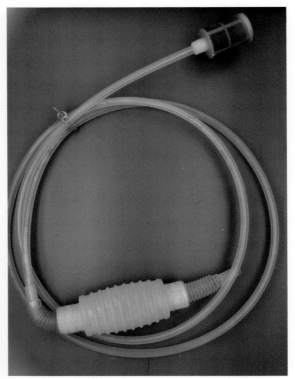

A siphon is a very enjoyable piece of kit to use, making a tricky job extremely simple. This version has a filter at one end – some demijohns have small necks and the filters don't fit through, in which case you'd have to do without this element.

A Wine Thief

This excellently named tool allows you to 'steal' a sample of liquid from your fermentation vessel with minimal disruption to either lees or vinegar mother. It's a plastic tube about 30cm in length with an opening at the top and a valve at the bottom that will allow the liquid to flow in when depressed. As you lift, the valve shuts, trapping the liquid inside. This is helpful for assessing specific gravity, pH, acidity and flavour. These are especially useful for deep vessels such as demijohns – other options are to use a turkey baster: I'd recommend a stainless-steel one as the glass versions are fragile – mine lasted about two days.

Ensure the wine thief has been sanitised (*see* page 41), then dip into the container to collect enough sample for your test. If all the equipment used for testing is clean, you can return the sample to the vessel afterwards.

Other Sundries

Other equipment might include electric weighing scales, for various weights, depending upon batch size – most domestic ones are up to 5kg, so if you are working with large quantities, you might need to borrow some. Also miniature scales for adding tiny quantities of yeast and nutrients, and commercial scales for quantities larger than 5kg, up to which regular digital domestic ones will be fine. Jugs with litre markings, a measuring cylinder and a selection of funnels will come in handy.

Notebook for Record Keeping

The more technical your approach, the more reproducible your vinegar will be, and probably the higher will be the concentration of acetic acid in your finished product (although there is a very wide range across which your vinegar will be delicious).

Jo Webster demonstrating the usefulness of a wine thief for sampling.

Of course, not every batch you make will be a triumph, especially if you're feeling experimental – over the years I have had issues with stuck fermentations, mould, recurring yeast pellicles, and red wine vinegar smelling like old socks. Using a notebook can help you spot what worked and what didn't. Make notes of everything: the source of the fruit or wine you are using, the temperature of the room, the sugar content, the starting pH, the ending pH, and so on. You don't have to do it manually, of course: the illustration shows a snapshot of the excel spreadsheet I use – you can embellish it however you see fit.

DATE	TYPE OF VINEGAR	ALCOHOL BASE	VOLUME	SG	Juice SG	Juice sugars	SUGAR/ I TO ADD TO 1.06	SG START	PH START	TEMP	PRIMARY	SECONDARY	END	FINAL SG	FINAL PH	ALCOHOL
12/10/2022	Quince	Juice	2L	1.035	91		132	1.056	3.6	RT	12/10/2022	17/10/2022	24/10/2022	1.005	3.3	0

This is a copy of the spreadsheet I use for alcoholic fermentation.

Masking Tape

Resist the temptation not to label things because you think you'll remember what it is… vinegar making from start to finish takes weeks, and trust me, you will forget! A roll of wide masking tape is a good solution for labelling things – it can be removed easily, and you can record lots of information on it – vinegar or wine type, start date, stage, pH, specific gravity and so on. This is better than writing directly on the bottle, as both alcohol and vinegar can dissolve pen on glass.

An Incubator

One of the most important factors influencing the speed of vinegar production is temperature, with about 28°C being optimal. You may find it desirable to control this unless you are prepared to wait extra months in a cold British winter. There are several choices: you can make your own incubator with a re-purposed polystyrene box and a thermostatically controlled heat mat, such as a reptile mat shown below. Cut out a channel for the cables. Do not stand the jars directly on the mat as this can cause hot spots and overheating – use a rack to stand the bottles on, or do as I have done and attach the mat to the lid instead.

You will thank yourself for recording this information…

You can make your own incubator from a simple re-purposed polystyrene box and reptile heat mat …

...or use a bread proofer.

Alternatively, you can buy a bread prover like the excellent collapsible machine by Brod & Taylor illustrated. It operates at the range preferred by vinegar microbes. You can even use it to make 'marmite' from the lees at its top temperature of 50°C.

If you're lucky enough to have more than one electric oven, the light on without any additional heat source may well provide the ideal temperature.

A Bottle of Vodka

Many a stubborn batch of vinegar has been enhanced, or starter revived, by the addition of a splash of alcohol. A bottle of vodka or other neutral source of distilled alcohol is a useful addition to your kit.

Thermometers

Temperature control can lead to better results. A digital room thermometer for working out the best spot for your ferments, and a food/drink thermometer for taking temperatures of musts and yeast preparations before the addition of yeast and/or measuring pH and specific gravity are useful.

LCD stick-on thermometers are ideal for the close monitoring of each batch, and a pan thermometer is invaluable for maintaining stove-top pasteurisation temperatures.

Straining Bags

Straining bags can make life easier, and nowadays can easily be found in most supermarkets in the produce section. If you place fruit or vegetable pulp in a straining bag before adding it into a bucket for primary fermentation, the process can still carry on, especially with daily stirring, and when it is time to remove the solids, it's as easy as lifting out the bag and waiting for it to drain. Don't squeeze too hard or you will let lots of tiny particulates back in, which could make the batch cloudy.

CLEANING YOUR EQUIPMENT

Ensuring that equipment is clean throughout the making process is of paramount importance. The presence of undesirable microbes at any stage could lead to spoilage or at the very least 'off' flavours, or problems with kahm yeast. A variety of cleaning methods can be applied, depending on what you are using; these are described below.

Cleaning Glassware

For smaller pieces of glassware, physically removing any debris followed by a hot dishwasher cycle will suffice, as these days most dishwashers end with a steam cycle.

If you don't have a dishwasher, hand washing in hot soapy water and thorough rinsing followed by microwave sterilisation is effective. It is difficult to give timings because microwaves vary so much in their efficiencies, and you may be sterilising several pieces at once. As a guide, ensure that the glassware is wet, but not dripping, and microwave until all water has evaporated – in my own machine this is 1.5min for a 1ltr mason jar. If you don't have a microwave, or if you are using glassware with metal fittings, oven heat at 160°C for 15min.

Always allow glassware to cool to below 30°C before using it. Cool liquid can crack hot glassware, and hot glassware can fry microbes. If you really are in a hurry, cool your glassware under hot running water first, and reduce the temperature of the water gradually.

Cleaning a Demijohn

Demijohns appear problematic to clean at first, with their inevitable tidemark that results from long fermentation times. However, there is a clever trick requiring a bottle brush with a long flexible handle: insert the brush into the bottle, and when you have done so, bend the handle at 90 degrees. You will then be able to clean the sloping sides of the jar with relative ease.

Demijohns are best sanitised with metabisulphite preparations (*see* below Cleaning Plasticware) because of their size.

Bending a flexible bottlebrush makes cleaning a demijohn light work.

Cleaning Glass Bottles

A similar trick helps keep vinegar storage bottles with a narrow neck clean. Sometimes a bottle brush on its own is not enough, and in these cases you will need a narrow strip of fabric that is about three times as long as the bottle height. Using a bottle brush, push the fabric into the bottle and move it round; this will remove stubborn debris more effectively.

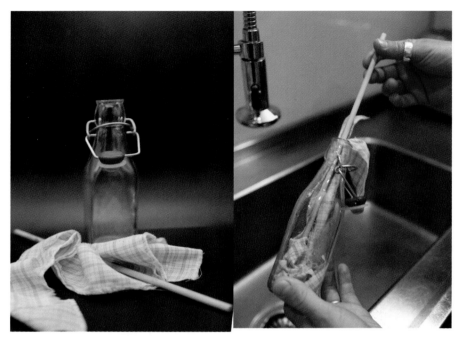

Vinegar storage bottles are often difficult to clean, but doing it this way has helped me save many of them from the recycling bin.

FOOD-SAFE DISINFECTANTS/ SANITISERS

Sanitisers tested to EN1276 and EN14476 standards are usually approved for commercial kitchen use. EntirePro EP0O4 is an example – it is fragrance free, non-tainting, and with a 30sec contact time. It can be used for cleaning hard surfaces and sanitising cloths and equipment.

'Magic Spray'
Turn to page 162 to find a home-made vinegar and alcohol-based recipe for a disinfecting formula.

Cleaning Plasticware

For vessels with hard-to-reach areas, or plasticware that can't be heated, chemical sterilisation is the way forwards. Campden tablets, or other makes of sodium metabisulphite, can be used for the sterilisation of demijohns and buckets for fermenting; SO_2 is the active agent, so use in a well-ventilated area. Another similar option is sodium percarbonate, which releases hydrogen peroxide. Anything submersible, such as plastic tubing or measuring cylinders, can be placed in a similar solution or in Milton fluid, and then left to drain and dry. In all cases, follow the manufacturer's instructions for making up solutions – they may vary, but it's very simple: just add the powder to water in the sink, and submerge what you're using in it for 10 to 20min. There is no need to rinse.

CHAPTER 6

HOW TO MAKE YOUR OWN VINEGAR

Given the abundance of AAB all around us, an open source of alcohol at the correct dilution may well turn to vinegar all by itself in time so we hardly need to intervene, but if we do, we can hone the process to influence flavour development, increase final acidity, and even speed things up.

WHERE TO MAKE VINEGAR

You don't need much room to make vinegar on a small scale – the simpler the set-up, the less space it will take. A single jar of a couple of litres capacity in a cupboard or on a work surface is all you will need. If you are

Making vinegar doesn't have to take up much space – just a litre jar on a shelf is a starting point...

... but it might grow into a bigger hobby!

HOW TO MAKE VINEGAR

ALL-IN-ONE

MAKE ALCOHOL
AND VINEGAR
AT THE SAME TIME

OR

TWO STAGE

MAKE OR BUY ALCOHOL.
SEPARATELY CONVERT
TO VINEGAR

ACETIFICATION (VINEGAR CONVERSION) METHOD
SURFACE PROCESS
CONTINUOUS CULTURE
BOERHAAVE PROCESS
MINI-TRICKLING GENERATOR
AERATION

CHOICES
WILD FERMENTATION OR ADDED CULTURES
TAKING MEASUREMENTS EG: pH, SUGAR, ACIDITY
ADDING NUTRIENTS, PECTINASE
PASTEURISING, AGEING, FILTERING

There are so many ways to make vinegar – it can be as easy or as complicated as you want. The more closely you monitor your brew, the more reproducible it will be, and the more predictable the outcome in terms of acidity.

making several barrels at a time, however, you will need to clear out the garage and provide some background heat for best results.

As figures above and below show, there are many paths to making vinegar – in fact if you add up all the permutations of methods and approaches, there are about fifteen!

The two approaches can be summarised as follows:

All-in-one: Left to its own devices, a simple preparation of juice or fruit pulp will turn itself to vinegar with little intervention other than the occasional stir. Naturally occurring yeasts will make

alcohol, while acetification by naturally occurring AAB occurs almost simultaneously.

Two-stage: This method separates out the two processes – either making your own alcohol or using a ready-made alcohol, and then a separate acetification step to make the vinegar. This allows much greater control and can lead to higher yields of acetic acid.

We shall start with the two-stage approach, as acetification of ready-made alcohol is the simplest and most direct way of making vinegar; it is also an excellent starting point for discussing parameters that affect the process, and how we can control them. We shall leave

There are about fifteen different combinations, if you consider making your own alcohol, not making alcohol, separate acetification, or all-in-one using various acetification systems – but use this chart to help you decide which one is compatible with your needs – and of course you can try them all!

Parameter/ Approach/Method	All-in-one	Surface	Continuous	Boerhaave	Trickling Generator	Aerated
Rapid				✓	✓	✓
Slow	✓	✓	✓			
One off batch	✓	✓		✓	✓	✓
Continuous	✓		✓	✓	✓	
Can be left		✓	✓		✓	✓
Needs daily attention	✓			✓		
Needs space					✓	✓
Fits anywhere	✓	✓	✓	✓		
Monitoring of parameters		✓	✓	✓	✓	✓
No monitoring	✓	✓	✓	✓		
Fruit Juice	✓	✓	✓	✓	✓	
Pulp	✓	✓				
Alcohol		✓	✓	✓	✓	✓

fruit preparation, all-in-ones and making alcohol bases until later in the book, but if you would like to jump ahead, please *see* pages 89 and 125.

THE TWO-STEP APPROACH

In the two-step approach alcohol is turned into vinegar.

Rudimentary Recipe

This rudimentary recipe is an excellent jumping-off point for starting your own vinegar production.

Using the surface method (*see* page 49), we will make a delicious, simple cider vinegar that can also be used as an active starter to inoculate any other vinegars you might make. I suggest that you set it up now, and as it becomes 'active' over the coming weeks, you can familiarise yourself with the rest of the book. When it's ready, you will be able to use it as follows:

- Use it all, for dressings, pickles, flavouring.
- Bottle some, and use the rest to make another batch.
- Make a continuous culture in a vessel with a tap for an everlasting, renewable supply.

You will need:

- 250ml of 5 per cent raw apple cider vinegar with the mother. Aspall, Willy's, Bragg, Sainsbury's Organic all work.
- 750ml of strong cider.
- A large 1.5ltr jar with a breathable cover (*see* page 34), or a fermentation box set up as on page 50.

Method:

- Shake the bottle of live vinegar vigorously for a few seconds to stir up the sediment and aerate.
- Add to the vessel with the cider and mix well. Cover. Leave for about six weeks somewhere not too sunny, between 21 and 28°C (28°C is optimal).
- Examine the jar weekly, but don't move it or you will disturb the mother of vinegar that will hopefully form across the top. At completion, there will likely also be sediment at the bottom.
- Taste it: if it tastes like vinegar, it is vinegar. Tip off 80 per cent and bottle it; use the remaining 20 per cent to start a new batch, either with or without the cellulose part.

STAGES IN VINEGAR PRODUCTION

DECIDE ON BASE ALCOHOL (YOURS OR READY-MADE)
↓
AMEND ALCOHOL CONCENTRATION TO SUIT THE AAB
↓
CHOOSE METHOD (ALL-IN-ONE, SURFACE, CONTINUOUS, BOERHAAVE)
↓
ADD ACTIVE VINEGAR MOTHER
↓
CHECK PH AND ACIDITY (OPTIONAL)
↓
INCUBATE
↓
CHECK WEEKLY/EVERY FEW DAYS
↓
IDENTIFY ENDPOINT BY TASTE/STABLE MEASUREMENTS
↓
FINISHING
↓
STORING

A summary of the stages in vinegar production.

Extending the Scope

Having seen how simple the process can be, we can apply the principle to other types of alcohol, controlling various parameters to ensure that a desired acidity of 5 per cent is achieved; also to influence the speed of vinegar production using various acetification methods.

The illustration above shows a flow diagram of the steps involved in more precise vinegar fermentation, which we shall then consider in turn.

CHOOSING AN ALCOHOL BASE

The more complex the alcohol base, the more flavourful your vinegar is likely to be. Home-made fruit wines are full of volatile organic compounds (VOCs), which can be further enhanced by acetic fermentation and subsequent ageing. Then there are thousands of ready-made sources, from liqueurs and spirits, finest champagnes to budget reds.

It really is this simple: cider and cider vinegar. You don't even need to de-gas it if you don't want to. Shake the vinegar, add, mix. You might never need to buy shop vinegar again! Use a medium sweet cider to encourage mother of vinegar growth.

There is a bewildering choice of alcohol with which to start your vinegar making – and they will *all* work! SHUTTERSTOCK

All wines must state their sulphite content if over 10ppm.

For best results choose a source with the following:

- An alcohol content of at least 6 per cent (to allow at least 4 per cent vinegar to be made, with production losses).
- No artificial colours or flavourings.
- A low level of sulphites.
- Some nutrients, including sugar (note: additional nutrients may be required for distilled spirits such as whisky, brandy, gin and vodka).

Sulphites

The term 'sulphites' refers to a range of sulphur-containing compounds, such as sulphur dioxide (SO_2) and sodium metabisulphite. Sulphites are a natural by-product of fermentation and act as preservatives, protecting against discoloration, oxidation and contamination. The process alone doesn't produce enough to preserve a wine indefinitely, so extra is often added. Sulphites have been used for centuries, their properties discovered when wine stored in pitch-lined amphorae was found to keep much better.

Any wine with more than 10ppm (parts per million) must state 'contains sulphites' on the label. In the EU, maximum levels are 210ppm for white wine, 400 for sweet wine and 160 for red wine. Red wine has lower levels because it contains tannins, which are natural antioxidants.

High levels of sulphite can inhibit AAB, so it is usually easier to make red rather than white wine vinegar. Your life will be easier if you can find some natural wine or cider without extra sulphite added.

If this isn't practical you have some choices:

- Accept that your fermentation will be slower.
- Use a step-wise inoculation procedure (*see* page 61).
- Try to remove them by one of the methods described below.

Hydrogen peroxide (H_2O_2): The addition of H_2O_2 oxidises sulphites to inactive hydrogen sulphate. Caution is required, however, because if you use too much you could generate sulphuric acid instead, which would not be ideal. This is complicated by the lack of precise sulphite content on wine bottle labels. I would recommend 0.5tsp 3 per cent hydrogen peroxide per 75cl bottle of wine. Mix well and leave for 30 minutes before use.

Aeration: Aerating the wine by pouring, stirring or using an air pump will help SO_2 to escape, but won't release sulphites that are bound to other components.

Gadgets: If you are intolerant to sulphites and already possess gadgets such as the Üllo wine purifier (£69.99 at the time of writing) or PureWine Wands, then these will help.

These devices are said to reduce sulphites via filtration.

All these vinegars have been made from bought wines.

Wine Vinegars

As wine quality and price are highly variable, how important is wine quality for vinegar making? As mentioned earlier, the process is extremely forgiving, the sourness of acetic acid masking all manner of ills, so I would suggest starting with less expensive blended wines to perfect your techniques, and then moving up the quality scale to see whether you can discern a difference. Almost all wines will need to be diluted before use to prevent alcoholic inhibition of fermentation (*see* page 49).

White Wine Vinegar

White wine vinegar is good to have on hand to inoculate other batches as it is fairly neutral in flavour and colour. I recommend keeping it in continuous culture (*see* page 83), then you can strain off and top up as required. If your white wine is very dry, you can add a little sugar to help the growth of mother of vinegar. Sauvignon Blanc does seem to make a particularly delicious version, especially mixed with sparkling water as a drinking vinegar (*see* page 158).

Red Wine Vinegar

Red wine turns more readily to vinegar than white, due to lower sulphite levels and the AAB growth-promoting properties of tannins; as seen in kombucha, SCOBY growth is more prolific in tea with high tannin levels. The vinegar has a reputation for having a hearty, unrefined flavour, and it is here that using smoother, more rounded wine, such as a merlot, could make a difference.

Don't forget to label it: it will be useful in the future!

Champagne, Prosecco, and Other Sparkling Wines
These will all make delicious vinegars. Although you might not want to break out the vintage Blanc-de-Blancs deliberately, the morning after a celebration, see what's left in the bottles, as leftovers can be used. Fizzy wines can be degassed before using, as high levels of CO_2 can inhibit vinegar production. Simply pour them into a jug and stir well, then leave until flat.

Using Cider and Beer as Bases

Try to choose varieties of cider and beer with a higher alcohol content to allow for dilution with vinegar mother and evaporation. Fizzy ciders and beers should be degassed, as above. If you have a favourite beer that is low in alcohol, add a neutral spirit to increase the level to 7 per cent.

Freezing Leftovers

If you don't have a continuous culture set-up, leftover wine can be frozen until you have enough for a batch of vinegar. Be sure to mark the alcohol percentage on the container you're storing it in, so you can dilute it as necessary when you come to use it.

CHOOSING AN ACETIFICATION METHOD

Converting alcohol to vinegar can be done in several ways, all based on those processes mentioned in the Introduction. There follows an explanation of each, with details of how to set them up, and the instructions for using them.

Surface Method (Batch Acetification)

Choose this method for low-intervention vinegar making with good flavour and bioactive component development. A batch of 7 per cent alcohol with 20 per cent vinegar mother starter is left at room temperature or warmer for several weeks, allowing acetification to take place. This can also form the basis for a continuous culture, but this is quite nuanced and has its own section later in the book.

Shallow systems acetify more quickly as there is greater access to oxygen, but are prone to greater

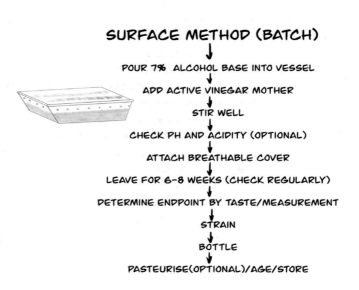

SURFACE METHOD (BATCH)
↓
POUR 7% ALCOHOL BASE INTO VESSEL
↓
ADD ACTIVE VINEGAR MOTHER
↓
STIR WELL
↓
CHECK PH AND ACIDITY (OPTIONAL)
↓
ATTACH BREATHABLE COVER
↓
LEAVE FOR 6-8 WEEKS (CHECK REGULARLY)
↓
DETERMINE ENDPOINT BY TASTE/MEASUREMENT
↓
STRAIN
↓
BOTTLE
↓
PASTEURISE(OPTIONAL)/AGE/STORE

Leave it alone, except for a weekly peep to see if the mother is developing. It doesn't always – but you won't want to miss it, because it's thrilling when it first happens.

Stages in preparation of a fermentation box, useful for small takeaway boxes, or for much sturdier, larger capacity glass boxes. First, heat a skewer, then pierce a plastic lid with a grid of holes. Apply a paper or cloth cover with glue.

evaporation. You can use any of the vessels already described – plastic buckets, glass vessels and so on (*see* page 33) – or for batches of 1 to 3ltr, why not make a fermentation box (*see* below)? Keeping to a depth of about 5cm in this set-up allows a good balance between acetification and evaporation. However, this would not be practical for larger volumes unless you can find very large, flat boxes.

Leave for four to six weeks, depending on temperature, and check weekly, though without disturbing the vessel, for the development of vinegar mother. When the mother has grown to the sides of the vessel you can leave it alone, as the concentration of volatiles of acetic acid within the air space will be high enough to prevent contamination.

Making a Fermentation Box
I like to use glass food containers with plastic lids – the ones from IKEA are perfect: robust and transparent. They are shallow, providing excellent surface area dynamics for fermentation and cellulose mother development. The lids can be easily manipulated to ensure sufficient but modified airflow, by piercing them with a heated skewer at 2cm intervals. I then apply either cotton fabric or robust kitchen towel over the surface using craft glue. Evaporation is reduced in comparison to using paper or fabric, especially at warmer temperatures. This is much easier than trying to fit a rubber band

and paper cover successfully over all corners of a large box.

HOME BOERHAAVE SET-UP

The theory is that by pouring your starter vinegar once or twice a day between two vessels, colonisation of the

The Boerhaave set-up: a few sticks are all you need. You can also use wood curls or chips if you prefer – the flow of air is the important thing.

wood by AAB and aeration will speed up the process, compared to a still, surface method. A reservoir of liquid is always present in the emptier jar, to prevent the sticks and microbes drying out.

You will need two 1ltr jars as a minimum, or up to 10ltr buckets, and some packing material. This can be twigs or beechwood shavings, or wood wool. Do check that your packing materials are food safe; I like using grapevines as they are readily available, harmless, and thin enough to be able to make a nice web as a supporting structure for the growth of microbes. You can also use woody herbal stems such as rosemary or thyme, although I haven't been overwhelmed with the amount of flavour they transfer. You will also need cloth or paper covers.

Choose twigs that are slightly shorter than the vessel and which therefore will not stick up through the paper. You can wash them and bake them in the oven for 15min at 160°C to kill any microbes or bugs that might interfere with the fermentation process, or you can use them as they are. When the twigs have cooled, soak them in some active raw vinegar for about an hour. Then transfer them to the jars, half in each. Don't worry too much about their arrangement. Fill one of the jars to about a quarter height with alcohol base and vinegar starter mixture, and pour the rest into the other jar. Apply covers to both jars. Once or twice a day remove the covers and tip all but 1/4 volume from the fuller vessel into the emptier one. At first you will need to put a clean hand or saucer over the top of the jar when tipping to prevent the sticks from falling out. After a few days this will cease to be a problem as they will be bound together with mother of vinegar.

Evaporation will occur during the process, so if you are hoping to end up with a litre, you would be wise to start with 1.2ltr.

For the first week or so you may find that little happens and all you can smell is damp wood. Keep going though, as one morning you will wake up to a web of AAB growing upon the surfaces of the grape wood and even across the top of the liquid. Fermentation will proceed much more quickly now; the turnaround time for this method can be as little as two or three weeks, compared to six to twelve weeks for a

THE BOERHAAVE METHOD

MIX 7% ALCOHOL BASE AND VINEGAR MOTHER STARTER
↓
CHECK PH AND ACIDITY
↓
ADD 1/4 TO ONE OF THE VESSELS
↓
ADD THE REMAINDER TO THE OTHER VESSEL
↓
ATTACH BREATHABLE COVERS
↓
DAILY, POUR THE FULLER JAR INTO THE EMPTIER JAR
↓
LEAVE 1/4 BEHIND EACH TIME (KEEPS WOOD MOIST)
↓
AFTER 3 WEEKS, TASTE AND/OR CHECK ACIDITY AND PH
↓
STRAIN TO REMOVE BITS OF WOOD
↓
AGE/PASTEURISE/STORE

Step-by-step Boerhaave instructions.

A web of mother is very easy to set up, but it becomes even easier when it forms and holds it together.

surface method. This system can be used permanently to make batch after batch – when vinegar mother growth becomes volume limiting, remove some of it. I keep my Boerhaave set-up on the go all the time.

This system is definitely happiest at 28°C, but it will function at room temperature, albeit more slowly.

THE TRICKLING GENERATOR

The Boerhaave method can be automated by combining packing materials with a re-circulation pump to make a version of the 'Trickly'. There is no official method for this, other than purchasing a

DIAGRAM OF A TRICKLING GENERATOR

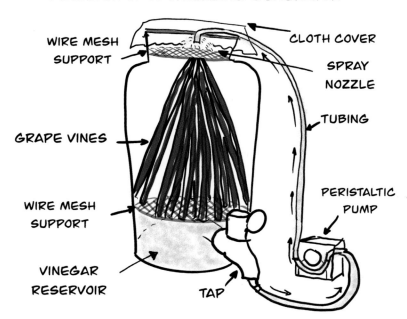

WIRE MESH SUPPORT

CLOTH COVER

SPRAY NOZZLE

TUBING

GRAPE VINES

PERISTALTIC PUMP

WIRE MESH SUPPORT

VINEGAR RESERVOIR

TAP

The simple equipment needed to automate the system.

How I set up the trickling generator – there is room for improvement and it is rather amateur, but it did the trick.

A nozzle was made by perforating the end of a felt-tip pen to create a spray.

Malle-Schmickl mini generator (998€). I have made my own fairly successfully, using some sheets of food-grade stainless-steel mesh, grape vines, some plastic line converters, tubing, and a peristaltic pump. I used the lid of a pen, which I perforated by piercing with a hot pin, to make tiny jets for the liquid to spray the wood. I found a conical arrangement of sticks to be most satisfactory, otherwise it was almost impossible to get coverage over the whole surface of the wood.

It certainly did speed up the process, and I had vinegar in about ten days, without the daily pouring of the Boerhaave method. I am sure that there are many ways of improving the system – I hope that you will be able to spend many happy hours developing these principles.

The idea is that the alcohol base is constantly recirculated over raw vinegar-soaked, AAB-inoculated sticks, keeping them constantly moist yet exposed to the air. Before setting up the system, you will need to measure how much liquid can be sequestered below the sticks – in my system it is 1.5ltr, so 1.5ltr is constantly recirculated. When it is time to check, you can detach the top tube to release some of the liquid. If it is ready, you can use the tap to decant the liquid, though you'll have to tilt it at a severe angle to drain it completely.

The generator, with its AAB-soaked branches, can then be used immediately for another batch. Getting it started is the same as for the Boerhaave method: simply add 1ltr (or more or less, depending upon the size of the reservoir you create) of 7 per cent alcohol and 20 per cent active vinegar mother starter, and turn it on.

AIR PUMP GENERATOR

Fish-tank air pumps can theoretically enhance the rate of vinegar production, passing oxygen continually through the system, partially mimicking the submerged process, without the automated stirring. Air pumps are discussed in more detail in the equipment section; there are factors influencing their utility.

The scientific literature[18] suggests that for maximum yield, flow rates between 0.25–1.5 vessel volumes per

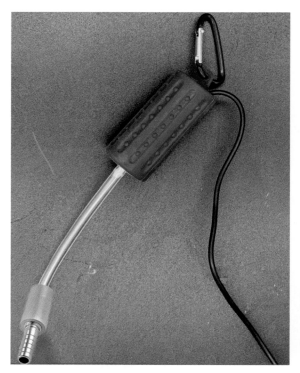

The equipment needed to aerate vinegar.

Build-up of mother on the airline using the air pump method. Remove this regularly to avoid over-oxidation hot spots.

hour (vvh) are required. For 1ltr that is 0.25–1.5vvh, or for 5ltr, 1.25–7.5vvh. Small air pumps are available with these outputs, however you might have to search them out.

Higher levels of aeration can be detrimental as they can increase the amount of evaporation – firstly of alcohol, the most volatile component of the system, but also of the vinegar itself. This can significantly decrease the yield of acetic acid, by as much as 25 per cent in my home experiments. The smaller the volume, the more marked this effect. For volumes less that 5ltr, if you can't reduce the flow rate to the required minimum, you could use a diverter to split the supply so that only a reduced volume of air enters the vessel.

The second issue is that after a few days, a mass of mother may begin to grow around the air stone, restricting the air flow, and will eventually need to be removed. If you leave it, it can actually cause a situation where over-oxidation occurs, and AAB can start to break down acetic acid in that area. I maintain that a trickling mini generator can give better results.

For this method, a bucket or glass vessel with a lid with a hole already in it for a fermentation valve would be ideal – you need a way of getting the air tube in without the fruit flies joining it, and it will decrease evaporation. Simply add 7 per cent alcohol with 20 per cent active vinegar mother starter to the vessel. Check for completion from five days. This will happen faster at 28°C.

CALCULATING THE CORRECT ALCOHOL CONCENTRATION FOR A BASE

As we have seen (*see* page 25), to achieve vinegar with 5 per cent acidity, a starting alcohol concentration of around 7 per cent is needed. It is easy to find ciders and beers around this level; these and home-made alcohol bases should not require diluting. Wines, fortified wines, spirits and liqueurs, however, will need to be. Use tap water, or fruit juice for more intense flavour, and add in your liquid vinegar mother starter too. I would not recommend diluting with fruit juice if you have an extremely acidic wine; the pH range for optimal action of AAB is over 3.5. Check with a pH meter if you're unsure.

(**Note:** Although opened undiluted wine can on its own turn to vinegar completely unaided, this can take months, as it requires a strain of AAB that is tolerant to high levels of alcohol to land in it, or for some of the alcohol in the wine to have evaporated first, allowing less tolerant strains to grow).

HOW TO MAKE 1L OF 7% ALCOHOL FROM VARIOUS % DRINKS

c1	c2	v2	v1	
Alcohol % of drink	Final required alcohol %	Volume of alcohol base	Volume of alcohol to add	Volume of water/ starter mix to add
10	7	1000	700	300
12	7	1000	583	417
15	7	1000	467	533
18	7	1000	389	611
30	7	1000	233	767
40	7	1000	175	825

How to make 1ltr of 7 per cent alcohol from different strength drinks. If it's not exactly the same as the one you're using, choose the nearest.

HOW TO CALCULATE 7 PER CENT STARTING ALCOHOL CONCENTRATION

These calculations for various alcohol percentages are based on making 1ltr alcohol base at 7 per cent concentration. If you need 2ltr you can double up, or for 5ltr times by five.

For greater accuracy, there is a formula for volume and concentration to help you work out how to dilute your chosen alcohol to a lower percentage:

$$V_1C_1 = V_2C_2$$

Which we can rearrange to: $V_1 = V_2C_2 / C_1$

V_1 is unknown (how much alcohol you need to add).

C_1 is the alcohol percentage of the drink we are diluting.

V_2 is the volume of alcohol base to vinegarise.

C_2 is 7 per cent (the target alcohol percentage I want in the base).

Here is an example:

I have some 18 per cent sherry that I want to turn into 1ltr (1,000ml) of 7 per cent alcohol base. How do I do this?

V_1 is unknown (how much sherry I need).

C_1 is 18 per cent (the alcohol percentage I have in the sherry).

V_2 is 1,000 (the volume of alcohol base that I want).

C_2 is 7 per cent (the target alcohol percentage I want in the base).

Substituting the numbers into the equation $V_1 = V_2C_2 / C_1$

$V_1 = 1,000 \times 7 / 18$

$V_1 = 389$ml of sherry are required.

I need to make this to 1ltr with water and vinegar mother, so…

1,000ml – 389ml = 611ml.

I will need to add 611ml water and vinegar mother combined.

The next step is to calculate how much vinegar mother to add.

For those averse to, or unsure of the mathematics, a general guide to dilution is shown in the illustration on the previous page.

If you'd like to work it out yourself, please *see* the box opposite.

ADDING MOTHER OF VINEGAR TO START FERMENTATION

As there is no natural source of AAB in bought alcoholic drinks, you will need to add some active vinegar starter – for example from the 'rudimentary recipe' on page 45. If you have made your own low-alcohol stock, there may well be active microbes still, so you can choose to wait and see, or go ahead and inoculate anyway.

A significant growth of mother can happen when you're not looking!

If you aren't concerned about the efficiency of the process or final vinegar acidity, you can be quite relaxed about how much to add, and 'some' starter will be sufficient – anywhere between 15 per cent and 30 per cent of the batch size. That means for a 1ltr batch, add 150–300ml. If you usually opt for 20 per cent you will be in the right ballpark.

If you are working with drinks with high levels of alcohol, you can include the starter in the liquid you will use to dilute it. This will help you maintain the ideal 7 per cent starting level. If your source of alcohol is already at 7 per cent you will be diluting it a bit, but don't worry too much – one of the reasons we are starting at 7 per cent to end up at 5 per cent is that a little dilution won't hurt – you are, after all, adding some acetic acid anyway in the starter, which will compensate.

(Further on in the book you will find the 'Stepwise' addition method that treats addition of starter vinegar quite differently – showing yet again that there is more than one way to make vinegar!)

Liquid versus Solid Mother

To seed a new batch, I usually use liquid starter; it is not necessary to include cellulose mother, although it does contain microbes. They usually sink anyway, and as mentioned earlier, can sequester oxygen from the system, slowing things down. In Boerhaave and generator set-ups, a lump of cellulose would just get in the way.

Maintaining Flavour When Adding a Starter

Especially when making more unusual vinegars, it is tempting to add minimal starter, to mitigate against adulterating the flavour that you're trying to develop. This is a valid concern. I have often added only a tiny splash of starter, thinking that I will end up with a more flavoursome final product, only to find that this slows the fermentation rate to the extent that you can lose more than you gain in evaporation. A better strategy is to add 20 per cent of a neutral raw vinegar – white wine, rice, or plain sugar water are good options. If an unusual vinegar is worth repeating, freeze some of it to use as a flavour-matched starter for the next batch.

CALCULATIONS FOR ADDING VINEGAR STARTER

A little extra precision can help your vinegar reach the correct final acidity. If you would like a guaranteed result, here are some calculations to help you in different scenarios:

Adding 20 per cent liquid vinegar mother starter when diluting an alcohol base to 7 per cent:

Carrying on from our sherry example on page 55, we have established that we need to add 611ml water and vinegar mother combined to 389ml sherry, to dilute the alcohol from 18 to 7 per cent.

I want 20 per cent (1/5) active vinegar starter in my batch. To work out how much that is, I must consider the batch size, which is 1ltr.

Using per cent calculations (per cent means fraction of a hundred):

$$20/100 \times 1000 = 200$$

I therefore need 200ml vinegar starter in the 611ml water/starter mix.

To work out how much water I also need, the calculation is as follows:

611ml–200ml = 411ml water (we can approximate – 400ml will do just fine).

Adding 20 per cent liquid starter without further dilution:

Assume I am making a litre of apple cider vinegar.

No dilution of alcohol content is needed, as it's already 7 per cent.

I need to add 20 per cent starter for the total volume:

20/100 × 1000 = 200ml starter

Adding 200ml starter to the 800ml = 1000ml. In this case, the starting alcohol concentration will be lower than 7 per cent as the starter has diluted it, *but* it will be adding in some acetic acid, so it compensates.

Adding cellulose mother:

I would recommend a 5×5×1cm piece of mother for every litre, but there is no particularly technical reason for this. Try to include at least some liquid too.

How to Add the Liquid Vinegar Mother Starter

Ensure that it is well mixed or shaken or contains liquid from both the top and bottom parts of a freshly growing batch. If taking from continuous culture, insert a long-handled spoon down the side to agitate the batch beneath the mother before drawing off with the tap. The most important thing is ensuring AAB are carried over. If using frozen vinegar ensure that it has thawed to room temperature. Simply shake and pour in the required amount, and/or throw in the cellulose mother and stir well.

CHAPTER 7

OPTIMISING ACETIFICATION

The vinegar-making process can be optimised in several ways, as described in this chapter.

OXYGEN

As AAB are obligate aerobes, making vinegar requires breathable systems. Some ceramic vinaigriers, mine included, come with lids that even though they are not air-tight, don't provide ideal circulation. You may smell an almost overpowering scent of pear drops or nail-varnish remover, which is symptomatic of low air flow – the two-stage acetic acid reaction can get stuck in the middle. Although it doesn't seem to affect the final acidity, it can slow down the vinegar process. Change to a cloth cap, or ensure that you regularly vent a ceramic or lidded jar.

For surface methods, as a rule of thumb try to maintain the ratio of a larger surface area relative to depth (*see* page 50). This won't be possible in all vessels: in a large deep tank, for example, some low-level aeration would be beneficial. As previously mentioned, air pumps can cause issues with over-evaporation, and sometimes over-oxidation of acetic acid can occur in low-ethanol pockets, especially with packing materials present. Always err on the side of caution and choose slower flow rates, rather than blasting with thousands of bubbles.

pH

Although AAB produce acid and have a moderate tolerance, their preferred working range is a strain-dependent pH 3.5–5.5.[18] Even though some wines are extremely acidic, with a pH as low as 2.9, upon dilution with water to get to a 7 per cent alcohol level, the pH nearly always ends up in range. If you are diluting with fruit juice, check with a pH monitor (*see* page 103) if your wine is pH 2.8 and the juice 2.9, say, as you will be making life hard for the AAB. Add less juice and more water. You could also add some food-grade potassium bicarbonate to raise the pH (follow the manufacturer's guidelines for quantities).

It is a good idea to record pH before fermentation begins, for troubleshooting down the line, and for tracking the end point.

TEMPERATURE

A stable temperature of 28°C is optimal, but in the UK this can be tricky to maintain in the long term unless there is an unusually hot summer. A digital thermometer placed in various locations at home will let you know if you have a suitable spot – for example an airing cupboard. Fermentation will occur at room temperature, but it will be slower. As acetic

Cashmere – what the best dressed vinaigriers are wearing this season.

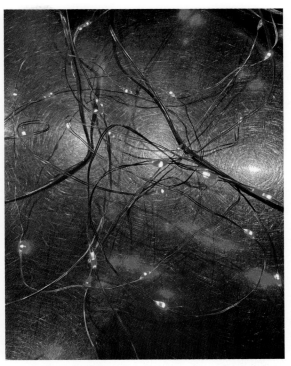

Research has shown that red light or darkness can slightly increase vinegar yield.

fermentation does produce a little heat, you could wrap your vessels in insulating fabric, or even crochet them little coats to capitalise on this and help keep them warm, or set up an incubator (*see* page 39).

LIGHT

It has been shown that acetic acid production by AAB differs according to the type of light source. Red LED lights increased the efficiency of the process,[19] compared to blue, green, white or non-LEDs. Other researchers found results comparable in the dark or with red light. Within my incubator I include a set of battery-operated red LEDs – I am not sure how much difference it makes but my vinegars seem very happy in there. It is not always possible to keep your vinegar in the dark, but do keep it out of direct sunlight. Glass jars can be painted with non-toxic paint, or covered.

NUTRIENTS

The must needs sufficient nutrients for the AAB to thrive, including the minerals magnesium and calcium. You can use a splash of beer, malt extract or raisins or dates to enhance an alcohol stock. Just tiny quantities are needed, but they can really help if your vinegar seems to be struggling to get going after a few days. This is especially necessary for spirit vinegar preparations that don't contain the bioactive components of wines, beers or alcohol bases.

EVAPORATION

The evaporation of alcohol is the enemy of the vinegar maker as it reduces the potential yield in terms of volume and acidity. Its effects are more marked in the warm conditions that speed fermentation, and with high humidity. This is in contrast to the evaporation of water, which reduces in a humid (saturated) environment. Alcohol is hydrophilic and is attracted to water droplets in humid air, thus creating a gradient so even more can leave the surface of the liquid. This makes management of evaporation extremely tricky, and explains why losses of up to 20 per cent can occur. A fermentation box with a vented lid will help balance airflow and evaporation loss (see page 50). If you are heating a cabinet with cloth or paper covers on the vessels, ensure that there is some ventilation to reduce humidity.

USING 'POTENTIAL ACIDITY' FOR ULTIMATE PROCESS CONTROL

Using 'potential acidity' for ultimate process control is the pinnacle of optimisation, a concept used in commercial production – however, you will need to be able to do acid/base titration for this method (see page 69). During fermentation, if the relative quantities of alcohol and acetic acid are maintained within certain limits, the fitness of the microbes can be optimised and efficiency increased.

We have already covered the 1:1 ratio between the amount of alcohol present and the acetic acid that can be produced (ignoring evaporation/microbial behaviour and so on) – for example, 5 per cent alcohol can theoretically produce 5 per cent acetic acid.

Because this is a one-way conversion, at any point the amount of acid and alcohol in the system can be added up to give the total amount of acetic acid that could be present in the final vinegar: we could say the potential acidity.

The table shows this alcohol:acetic acid ratio at various stages, assuming 5 per cent alcohol to start, and adding 20 per cent v/v of 5 per cent acetic acid starter.

Vinegar experts Malle and Schmickl have determined that vinegar formation is expedited by several days when the initial alcohol:acidity ratio is approximately 2:4 – that is, 2 per cent alcohol and 4 per cent acidity.[20]

After a few days' fermentation, when the microbes are flourishing, they can tolerate the addition of higher alcohol levels. Two or three gradual additions of alcohol base can lead to faster fermentation times and higher yields, as opposed to overwhelming the microbes all at once. You can keep making further stepwise additions to make vinegars of up to 10 per cent, until the AAB cannot cope with the acidity.

Time point	Ratio alcohol:acetic acid
Before inoculation of alcohol base with vinegar starter	5:0
After adding a known % acidity of starter (5%)	5:1
As the reaction proceeds:	4:2
Now the amount of alcohol and acetic acid is equal	3:3
Now the amount of alcohol is less that the acetic acid	2:4
Now the conversion is almost complete	1:5

Potential acidity of a system: how the amount of alcohol and acetic acid present can be used to determine the total potential acetic acid concentration.

This can be done with great accuracy via measurement of both acidity and alcohol levels; however, as alcohol measurement for the home fermenter is almost impossible, we shall apply the principle in a more relaxed fashion, simply adding portions of alcohol base in two stages a couple of weeks apart. I would, however, recommend starting off at the suggested 2:4 alcohol:acidity ratio, which can be calculated if your alcohol and vinegar concentrations are known (use commercially available ones if you are not sure).

Setting up a Stepwise Starter

This works most effectively when at 10 per cent of the final volume, so 200ml would be required for a 2ltr batch of vinegar.

Ingredients to provide the 2:4 alcohol:acetic acid ratio:

- 160ml of 5 per cent active vinegar mother starter.
- 10ml spirit alcohol – for example, vodka – at 40 per cent.
- 30ml water.

To see the maths behind these calculations, or to use your own alcohol/vinegars at other concentrations, *see* the box below.

Method:

- Combine the ingredients and put in a vented fermenting box, up-and-running Boerhaave set-up, or mini-generator at 28°C (we are aiming for optimal conditions).
- After four days, carry out a titration to assess the concentration of the batch. The amount of acetic acid should have increased from 4 per cent to 5 per cent as the alcohol (which we are not measuring) should have decreased from 2 per cent to 1 per cent.
- If it has not, try again after another 48 hours.
- When this point has been reached, the microbes can be challenged with a higher level of alcohol. Add half of the remaining 7 per cent alcohol base and ferment for fourteen days.
- Add the final portion and ferment for a further fourteen days.
- Check final concentration by titration if desired – you should have top-quality vinegar within five weeks.

CONCENTRATION CALCULATIONS

We have already come across the formula $V_1C_1=V_2C_2$ to dilute the concentration of a solution (on page 55), which has been used to calculate how much alcohol to add above. Sometimes, however, it is necessary to increase the acidity of a starter by adding some stronger vinegar to fortify it. This requires a different approach. You can substitute your own values in the table below or, alternatively, visit the 'mixing vinegar calculator' at making-vinegar.com and substitute your values in the boxes. Here is an example of how to calculate it yourself. Let us work out what quantities must be added together to increase the acidity of a 3 per cent starter (A) using 6 per cent distilled vinegar (B), to make 200ml of 4 per cent vinegar (C):

Mixing Vinegar Calculations

The amount of Vinegar A + Vinegar B = Vinegar C so solving for x,

$3(200 - x) + 6x = 4(200)$

$600 - 3x + 6x = 800$

$600 + 3x = 800$

$3x = 800 - 600$

$3x = 200$

$x = 200/3$. Therefore **x = 66**

66ml of vinegar B and 200 – 66ml = 134ml of vinegar A, when mixed together, will make 200ml of 4 per cent vinegar starter.

	CONC.	AMOUNT	Value = CONC. x AMOUNT
Vinegar A	3%	200 – x	3 (200 – x)
Vinegar B	6%	x	6x
Vinegar C (target)	4%	200	4 (200)

SIGNS OF ACETIFICATION

What to Look For as Fermentation Proceeds

With surface methods, depending upon the temperature, an almost imperceptible film will form across the top of the liquid, within either a couple of days or a couple of weeks. At first it might look like separate colonies of something suspect, but it will be shiny in the light. Gradually it will coalesce. With generators, aerated systems or Boerhaave methods, the mother won't get a chance to settle across the top, and the solution will clear either completely or partially as fermentation proceeds. If anything untoward appears, see page 76.

Spotting the Endpoint of Vinegar Fermentation

A combination of visuals, smell, taste and measurements will help determine when your vinegar is done.

Do check progress regularly but without disturbing a forming mother. You can use a pipette, turkey baster or straw with a finger over the end to withdraw some fluid from the side of it, or a wine thief for large batches. Vinegar smells astringent, and not alcoholic. When it's done the aroma may even make you cough and your eyes water. To assess by taste, for batch vinegar, dip a finger in a sample that has been removed from the vessel so as not to contaminate it. If it is continuous culture vinegar, or stepwise vinegar that is likely to be upwards of 6 per cent, dilute it 50/50 in a little water before tasting in case it's unpleasantly strong.

Visually, vinegars are nearly always clearer than starting musts, with lees usually present at the bottom of the fermenting vessel – not to the extent of wine lees, but evident.

If smell, taste and appearance tick all the boxes, you can go straight to finishing off (see below, page 63) or bottling (page 66).

For greater precision, monitoring the process and recording data will help you identify the endpoint and will be useful for subsequent batches. Monitoring points will vary according to the method used:

Slow surface: Leave for three weeks, then examine weekly.

Continuous: Weekly.

Stepwise at 28°C: Every four days.

Boerhaave: Every three days.

Generator: Every three days.

At each time point, measure the pH, acidity, and a hydrometer/alcoholometer relative reading (see the next section on page 67). Record these in a notebook or spreadsheet, or you can stick a label on to the vessel or cupboard door if you'd prefer to note them down quickly. When the values stop changing, it's a good indication that the vinegar is ready.

The start of the formation of vinegar mother is almost impossible to photograph – these very different examples are all newly forming mother.

FINISHING OFF

When your vinegar is ready, remove any cellulose (*see* page 29 for how to store). Transfer to sterilised bottles of your choice (*see* page 66), or carry out any of the procedures described below.

Clarifying your Vinegar

Filtering
Vinegar can often be cloudy. This will depend upon the fruit that was used and how much pectin it contained, or other compounds that lead to cloudiness that cannot always be predicted. If your vinegar contains lots of bits of mother and has been through the Boerhaave process with sticks or wood chips you will probably want to filter, using a fine sieve at first, and then, if you have the patience, a coffee filter for small volumes, or a professional-grade filter for better

Cloudiness is a natural feature of some vinegars, like the persimmon on the left. The ACV on the right is made from low-pectin dessert apples and is clear.

results and larger volumes. I do not often filter other than sieving; upon bottling, there will be further settlement of sediment over some weeks. When you filter a vinegar, you are no doubt removing some of the additional qualities too.

Note that filtering will not remove all the AAB. The process is not sufficient to pasteurise or completely stabilise your vinegar.

Another way to clarify vinegar is to freeze and then thaw it. This can lead to sedimentation of particles, which can be left behind when the vinegar is decanted to a new sterile container.

Fining
You may have heard this term in connection with wine. It is a process of clarification and stabilisation, requiring the addition of fining agents – compounds that interact with and remove tannins, polyphenols and proteins. I'm quite sure that you wouldn't want to add fining agents such as gelatine, food-grade charcoal, egg white or bentonite to your vinegars – nor would I recommend it, as the compounds you would be removing are the very ones that make your vinegar better than the shop version.

Pasteurisation
Pasteurisation will ensure the enduring stability of your vinegar. It will terminate the AAB, and there will be no risk of bacterial over-oxidation. From this point forwards it will not be live, and so will not be able to start fermentation in another batch. The advantages are that your vinegar will retain its quality for longer, as no low-level biological changes will occur. Pasteurised vinegar can still be aged.

Louis Pasteur invented the thermal process that now bears his name. This mild heat treatment of food kills potential pathogens without altering the flavour or the nutritional content too much. It works by denaturing enzymes that are essential for bacterial growth and reproduction and is responsible for damaging cell walls.

It is effective against microbes that do not form spores, including yeasts, *Acetobacter* sp., *E. coli*, *Listeria monocytogenes*, *Campylobacter* and *S. aureus*: pasteurised milk even refrigerated will eventually go off, while spore-forming *Paenibacilli* survive pasteurisation and will eventually germinate and spoil the milk.

There are different ways of achieving pasteurisation, either 'high temperature short time' (HTST) or 'low temperature long time' (LTLT). HTST requires heating to 71.5°C for 15 to 30sec and then cooling rapidly to 4–5.5°C. This method is commonly used in industrial settings, as it is difficult to achieve such rapid heating and cooling in a home environment.

LTLT requires heating to 63°C for 30min, followed by rapid cooling, which is more manageable at home. There are several ways to go about this – the most difficult thing is maintaining the temperature.

Stove-Top Pasteurisation

Heat a saucepan of water to 63°C: the water should be at least as deep as the liquid level in your bottles. If necessary, stabilise them with a tea towel, or another vessel to stop them bobbing about and falling over. Attach a thermometer to the side of the saucepan, or stick a digital one in the top of one of the bottles. Maintain the temperature for 30min. This will be easier with a heat diffuser on most stovetops. I don't usually put the lids on, but you can add them loosely if you wish. If you want to pasteurise before bottling, use a double boiler – a bowl within a bowl – to stop the vinegar at the bottom of the pan from overheating.

Instant Pot/ Thermomix

If you are lucky enough to have a newer model Instant Pot, the 'keep warm' function has a pre-set temperature of 63°C. Either pasteurise liquid directly in the pot, or heat water first and add bottles containing vinegar. Do check first as my own, older machine is much hotter than this. A Thermomix can be used to maintain temperature within a narrow range with stirring for liquid only that can then be transferred to sterilised bottles.

Oven Pasteurisation

Heat moves more efficiently through water than through air, so for oven pasteurisation a higher temperature is required: 120°C fan or 130°C conventional for 30min, or to be more thorough, prepare a water bath that you can put in the oven that is at 63°C, into which you can place the bottles.

An instant pot, Thermomix or large saucepan can all be used to maintain pasteurisation temperature. Pack the bottles in quite tightly so they don't fall over when you add the water.

Cooling the Bottles

Cap bottles, or place liquid in sterile bottles and cap, then cool rapidly by transferring to a sink of cold water. I would add ice after an initial cooling to avoid thermal shock to the bottles.

Ageing

Storing your vinegar for some weeks before using it can intensify the flavours, for both raw and pasteurised vinegars. It is likely that a slow Maillard reaction carries on with traces of protein, forming new flavour, compounds. Beneficial developments are more marked when vinegar is stored in wooden barrels, which, as we will see, is how both sherry and balsamic vinegars are made. In the latter case, a series of barrels of different woods are used, adding levels of complexity at each stage. If you are lucky enough to have a wooden barrel in which to store your finished vinegar, seal it completely, unless you wish to add more alcohol and undertake further fermentation, to intensify the flavour (remember this will not work with pasteurised vinegar).

Wood chips range from deliciously scented pieces of old whisky barrel to sawdust and beech chips. You can smoke the wood first if you like.

You don't need as many wood chips as you might think – follow the recommendations on the packet. Also, they often float!

A short cut is the addition of food-safe wood chips. These are commonly used in smoking and are available online, just like those that can be used for the Boerhaave process. A recent study showed that wood-aged vinegar contained higher levels of polyphenols and other bio-actives than non-wood aged.

You don't need to add as many as you think for ageing – it's rather different to the Boerhaave process. Add the recommended amount for the type you buy – there's a whole range from sawdust to big lumps. I added a teaspoon of chips to this mixed vinaigrier vinegar (pictured below) and within just a few days, the difference in flavour was profound – intense and delicious! The chips float for a couple of days, but soon sink to the bottom. It is definitely recommended.

Smoking Vinegar

Cold-smoking vinegar is remarkably effective, especially with herb-infused or rich red vinegars. Simply pour into a flat, food-safe container for maximum exposure and place in the cold smoker for 24 hours. Bottle and store, with as little air in the bottle as possible.

Can Vinegar Go Off?

The answer to this is unhelpfully yes and no. Industrially made and pasteurised white distilled vinegar is likely to last for years – even though it will have a 'best before' date, this is really to protect manufacturers from consumers returning ten-year-old bottles.

Other industrially produced non-live vinegars – malt, for example – will last a similarly long time, but you might notice some differences in appearance over several years. If you have a very old malt vinegar in the cupboard, go and examine it – there may well be sediment at the bottom, and it may have lightened in colour; and if it is white balsamic vinegar, it can sometimes undergo a slow Maillard reaction if sugars and amino acids are present and darken over time. None of these issues will affect the acetic acid concentration, and it will remain safe to use.

If home-made live vinegar at 5 per cent acidity is pasteurised it will last indefinitely, apart from undergoing slow flavour enhancing/changing reactions. Lower acidity vinegar could potentially be at risk of spoilage.

Raw, live, unpasteurised vinegars behave differently, as they contain still-living micro-organisms that can affect the composition of your vinegar in the long term. If oxygen is allowed in the storage vessel, in the absence of any residual alcohol, AAB will eventually

Two identical balsamic vinegars; the darker one is two years older than the lighter.

Having a very small opportunity for oxygen exchange means better preservation of the vinegar.

begin to oxidise their own acetic acid to carbon dioxide and water. This will lower the acidity and raise the pH, leaving the vinegar vulnerable to contamination.

How to Store Vinegar Correctly

To avoid these issues, live vinegar should be kept in a low oxygen environment – tall, narrow bottles such as the ones used by the Slow Vinegar Company are ideal, as they have very little surface area for oxygen exchange. An alternative method is to reduce the bottle size as you use the vinegar – this way you can keep it alive without risk of oxidation.

For 75cl quantities, I particularly like corked spirit bottles with heavy bases because they are so aesthetically pleasing, though they are large and not particularly suitable if you leave them half empty. I would decant into smaller bottles as the amount of air increases, unless the vinegar is pasteurised. 100ml clip-top bottles are perfect for presents – look out for suitable bottles of varying sizes, ask your friends – you might find lovely specimens in second-hand shops, but remember that ornamental glass may not be food safe.

Vinegar, especially live vinegar, is best maintained at a cool room temperature away from direct sunlight. It can be refrigerated to slow its microbial degradation. However, upon doing so, many of the volatile substances that provide the complex flavours can become extremely subdued, and I would recommend allowing it to come to room temperature before using.

These solid-based corked bottles are a good choice – and very easy to get hold of too – ask your friends to keep them.

CHAPTER 8

MONITORING ACETIFICATION

While people have been making vinegar for centuries without these analyses, and you are quite at liberty to carry on that great tradition, it is both helpful and (in my opinion) fun to monitor your vinegar's progress and its final 'vital statistics'. The two most useful parameters are pH and acidity.

USING PH TO MONITOR ACETIFICATION

Use pH to determine the starting pH of a vinegar fermentation, as an adjunct to determining the endpoint of vinegar fermentation and also to determine whether something has gone awry.

At the time of writing, an entry level pH meter is about £12, and a more reliable one about £30. These devices are also invaluable if you are interested in vegetable fermentation. Because a roll of hard-to-interpret universal indicator paper costs about £6, I would recommend purchasing a meter. It must be calibrated before use, using buffer solutions at known pH (usually pH 4 and pH 7), to ensure accurate readings. If you only use it occasionally, you should calibrate it every time. pH is temperature sensitive. If you feel like splashing out, some meters automatically adjust the reading according to the temperature, or you will need

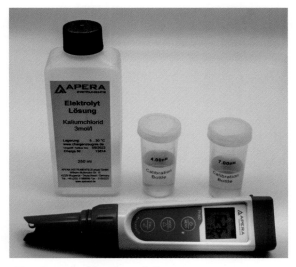

pH meter and calibrating solutions.

to make sure that your calibration and test solutions are all at 20°C.

Always make sure that you clean and dry a pH meter carefully between testing different solutions and after use; do not allow matter to build up on the electrode. The ends are vulnerable to damage, so treat them gently. Store it in the suggested storage solution, which is usually 3M potassium chloride. Always follow the instructions for your device.

The pH Scale

pH, where the p probably stands for potential and the H definitely stands for Hydrogen, is a concept developed over 100 years ago by Danish chemist S. P. L. Sørensen, to determine the acidic or basic (alkaline) nature of aqueous solutions.

Acids are substances that can release hydrogen ions (H+) in aqueous solutions, whilst bases release hydroxide (OH–) ions. If a solution contains more H+ ions it will be acidic: if it contains more OH– ions it will be basic. If it contains equal numbers of H+/OH– it will be neutral.

The pH scale operates between 0 and 14, where 0 is extremely acidic, 14 is extremely alkaline and 7 is neutral. The scale is logarithmic, which means that numbers with lots of decimal places are hidden behind the seemingly simple scale; a solution at pH 3 contains 0.001 moles of hydrogen ions per litre and is 1,000 times more acidic than a solution at pH 6, which contains 0.000001 moles of hydrogen ions per litre. pH meters measure hydrogen ion concentration using the potential difference of the test solution compared with an internal reference.

The pH scale can describe the concentration of free, detectable hydrogen ions in solution. It cannot detect them if they are bound to other molecules. To determine how much acetic acid has been made during fermentation, measuring pH isn't enough; although the pH will show a low reading, somewhere between 2.5 and 3.5, it can't tell you how much is present.

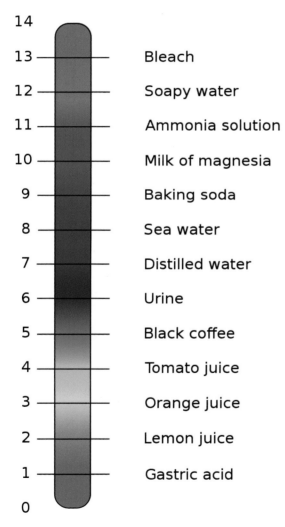

The pH levels of some common substances; vinegars are usually in the range of pH 2.8 to pH 3.6, but are always well below neutral unless something has gone awry – in which case they are no longer vinegar! Wikimedia commons Edward Stevens

The Difference between pH and Titratable Acidity (TA)

To reiterate, the pH of a solution is a measure of the concentration of free hydrogen ions in solution. This can be affected by dissociation of weak acids and buffering by other substances that can 'soak up' hydrogen ions, which is especially likely to happen in complex home-made vinegars. But the acid it still there: we can still taste it.

It is helpful, and in some cases essential, to know how much of it there is: to be sure that your vinegar is acidic enough to be used safely for food preservation, an accurate measure of the concentration of acetic acid per litre is required (in the UK this is 5 per cent w/v acetic acid). This is also important as the perception of acidic flavour can be strongly influenced, or masked, by the presence of sugars.

Titratable acidity, which I also like to think of as 'tasteable acidity', is a test that can measure all hydrogen ions present, whether or not they are dissociated. We can use this to find the concentration of vinegar.

Unfortunately there is not a clear relationship between the pH and TA in wild vinegars. You could have a vinegar with a pH of 2.8 and a TA of 2.5 per cent, or a vinegar with a pH of 3.3 and a TA of 5 per cent. It depends on the complexity and composition of the vinegar in question, the amount of buffering, other compounds present, and so on. If you kept making the same vinegar, in the same conditions, you just might be able to work out a reliable relationship through rigorous repetition of measurements.

Shop-bought white distilled vinegar is a simpler proposition, as it is made from a pure distilled alcohol base. Its pH can be reliably predicted at 5 per cent acetic acid w/v to be pH 2.8.

ACID-BASE TITRATION

If you are regularly assessing acetic acid concentration, I recommend investing in your own set-up, which is also a fantastic opportunity to play at being a kitchen scientist. It is accurate, and cheaper than buying ready-made kits or sending samples to the lab for gas chromatography analysis. Given the number of pages dedicated to this section, it might seem like a daunting proposition – however, the more you do it, the easier it becomes.

Acid-base titration is a clever way of working out an unknown amount of a substance, in this case acetic acid, using information contained within a chemical formula and a known amount of another substance, a base, in this case sodium hydroxide (NaOH).

When an acidic solution meets a basic one, at some point there will be a neutralisation reaction – they will cancel each other out. With an appropriate colour-changing reagent, you can spot when this point occurs. The equation below shows that one mole (one quantity) of acetic acid neutralises one mole (one quantity) of sodium hydroxide. If the quantity of NaOH is known, the amount of acetic acid to neutralise can be calculated.

Note: Although this reaction is not specific for acetic acid, small quantities of other organic acids are likely to be present in home-made vinegars, but we can assume that it is going to account for almost all of it.

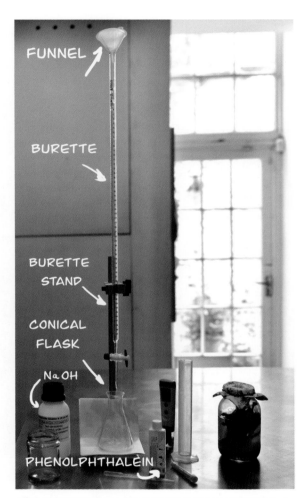

All the kit you will need in order to carry out a titration. A burette might seem unnecessary, but they are great fun to use, and not particularly costly. You could instead use more concentrated 1M NaOH, and use a syringe to add to a conical flask. You would probably need to add up to 5ml.

EQUATION FOR THE REACTION BETWEEN ACETIC ACID AND SODIUM HYDROXIDE

$$CH_3COOH + NaOH \longrightarrow CH_3COONa + H_2O$$

The equation that governs the neutralisation reaction between acetic acid and the base, sodium hydroxide. At the neutralisation point, the amount of acid and base present will be equal. We know how much base (NaOH) we have, so can use this to work out how much acetic acid is present.

You will need the following equipment:

A burette
A burette stand
A measuring cylinder
A small funnel
A conical 200ml flask (or a jam jar)
Phenolphthalein indicator
Sodium hydroxide solution (0.1M or 1M)
A plastic pipette
A glass beaker (or a jam jar)
Calculator or spreadsheet

A 10ml syringe
A piece of white card
A pair of safety goggles
A pair of laboratory gloves
A pinny
A pH probe if you are titrating a dark-coloured vinegar

All the equipment is easily and economically available on eBay or at other online retailers, and reagents at APC Pure (*see* page 172). Assemble the apparatus as shown in the illustration below.

(A) Don your safety glasses and fill the burette with sodium hydroxide to a few ml above 0. (B) Run some through the nozzle by turning the tap until it gets to 0 – make sure you get rid of any air bubbles. (C) Ensure the meniscus is at 0. (D) Place your 6ml sample with some water in the conical flask. (E) Add a couple of drops of indicator. (F) Using the tap, run the sodium hydroxide into the conical flask, swirling constantly. (G) When it turns this pale pink, the equivalence point has been reached. (H) Read the level in the burette. In this example the meniscus is at 28.2 – I used 6 per cent sample size and 0.1M NaOH, so this tells me I have only 2.82 per cent acetic acid in the sample – very weak vinegar!

Notes

- If you record the quantities, it doesn't matter how much vinegar, or what concentration of NaOH you use, as the calculations can be altered accordingly. However, *I strongly recommend that you test exactly 6ml of vinegar. If you do this, the reading on the burette will be the same as the acidity. You might have to move a decimal point depending on the concentration of NaOH used, but it will save a lot of maths!*
- I prefer to use 0.1M NaOH, because I am accident prone, and anything stronger can cause burns. The downside is that using weak NaOH means that you will use a lot more of it, and you will need to divide the amount of NaOH by ten to get the correct answer! If you are calm and careful, you may prefer to use a more concentrated solution, but always wearing gloves and goggles.
- The first time you do this, I would recommend trying it out with a shop-bought vinegar of known acetic acid concentration – most likely 5 per cent w/v. This will provide a reference point, and you will be able to check that your calculations are correct.

Method

- Using the measuring cylinder and funnel, pour sodium hydroxide solution of known concentration into the burette. Over-fill slightly past the zero mark, and then run some through into a beaker, making sure that the meniscus ends up at zero and that the tap section of the burette is full.
- Use the syringe to put exactly 6ml test vinegar into the conical flask.
- Add 20ml water (this is not critical – it will not affect the molecules of acetic acid you're detecting; it just provides a volume of liquid so you can see the colour change).
- Add two drops of phenolphthalein indicator solution with a pipette.

- Place the white card on the stand, and position the conical flask under the burette.
- Start adding NaOH to the conical flask, swirling with one hand and using the tap with the other hand. The stronger the NAOH, the less you will need to neutralise the acetic acid.
- When you are approaching the neutralisation point, the pink colour of the phenolphthalein will stay for a few seconds before dissipating.
- Add NaOH now drop by drop until the whole contents of the flask turns a pale pink. The neutralisation point has been reached.
- Write down the amount of NaOH you have used.

Calculating the Concentration of Acetic Acid

With a 6ml sample size of test vinegar:
If you used 1M NaOH, the reading in the burette is the same as the acidity: 4.9ml of NaOH means the acidity is 4.9 per cent w/v.

If you used 0.1M NaOH, the reading in the burette needs to be divided by 10: 44.5ml means that the acidity is 4.45 per cent.

If you would like to understand the maths behind these calculations, or stubbornly refuse to use a 6ml sample size, please *see* below.

Titrating Coloured Vinegars

If you are titrating red wine or beetroot vinegar, you will not be able to see a pale pink colour change, even if you only use a couple of ml to test. However, there is another way: place your pH probe in the conical flask as you swirl. When you reach a pH of 8.6, this is the neutralisation point. You might notice that a greyish colour change also occurs. Write down the amount of NaOH used.

You may be wondering why the point of neutrality doesn't occur at pH 7, which of course we know to be neutral pH. The reason is that at the equivalence point, all the acetic acid has reacted with sodium hydroxide, creating a conjugate base, sodium acetate, which is basic, so the pH is above 7.

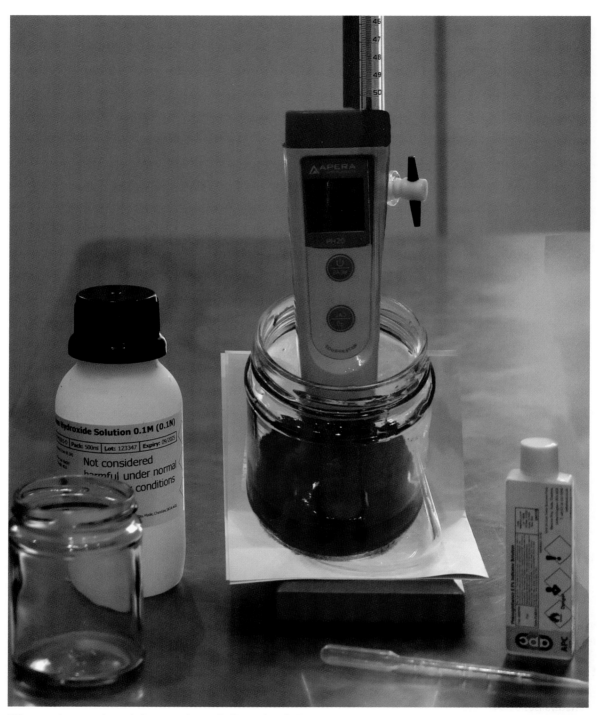

When you have a coloured vinegar, using an indicator is pointless. Here you must rely upon your pH meter to tell you when you have reached pH 8.6 – the equivalence point.

WHAT IS A MOLE?

A mole is a standard scientific unit used for measuring large quantities of very small things such as atoms or molecules. It means the amount of substance that contains 6.02×10^{23} particles, as determined by a scientist called Avogadro. It's a way of comparing dissimilar things. It's rather like having a dozen oranges and comparing that with a dozen M&Ms, or a dozen chickens. You have a dozen of each, but they are different things.

A mole of a substance (in grams) is numerically equal to its molecular weight.

One mole of CH_3COOH weighs 60.05g.

There are two carbon atoms (molecular weight approximately 12g/mol), four hydrogen atoms (1g/mol) and two oxygen atoms (16g/mol). Adding these together, acetic acid has a molar mass of 60.05g/mol.

One mole of NaOH weighs 40g. (One sodium atom (23g/mol), one hydrogen atom (1g/mol), and one oxygen atom (16g/mol)).

In our alcohol equation,

$$C_6H_{12}O_6 \rightarrow 2C_2H_5OH + 2CO_2$$

We can see that one mole of glucose breaks down to two moles of ethanol and two moles of carbon dioxide. How can this happen? Well, the glucose molecule is very large, and all of the C, H and O can be rearranged to make two lots of ethanol and two of carbon dioxide.

TITRATION CALCULATIONS

If you are using a sample size other than 6ml for your titration, here is an example showing the steps to calculate the w/v acetic acid concentration:

$$CH_3COOH + NaOH \rightarrow CH_3COONa + H_2O$$

My test solution is 5ml of a vinegar I have made, and I am titrating with 0.1M NaOH. I carry out the titration. The amount of 0.1M NaOH used to neutralise the test solution is 42.8 ml.

The first stage is to calculate the number of moles of NaOH used. Using the green triangle:

Moles NaOH = Molar conc. × volume used (in litres or dm^3)
Moles NaOH = 0.1×0.0428
Moles NaOH = 0.00428

From the equation, we see that the moles of NaOH and CH_3COOH used are the same (one of each), so we can deduce that 0.00428 moles of NaOH neutralises 0.00428 moles of CH_3COOH.

Using the orange triangle, and knowing the molar mass of CH_3COOH (60.052; *see* above box on moles), we can calculate the mass of acetic acid present:

Mass of CH_3COOH = Moles x Molar Mass
Mass of CH_3COOH = 0.00428×60.052
Mass of CH_3COOH = 0.257

Our 5 ml test sample contains 0.257g. For a w/v percentage we need to calculate this per 100 ml:

5 ml contains 0.257g
100 ml contains $100/5 \times 0.257 = 5.14$g

Therefore, the acidity of the vinegar sample is 5.14% w/v.

NB: if a v/v concentration were required, a density calculation would also be necessary. In the UK, however, vinegar concentration is measured w/v (according to trading standards).

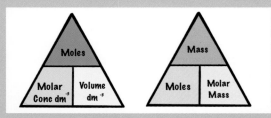

These triangle formulae can be used to work out molar concentrations; moles = molar conc dm^{-3} × volume dm^{-3} and mass = moles × molar mass. NB: $1dm^3$ = 1 litre.

ALCOHOL DETECTION IN PROGRESSING OR FINISHED VINEGAR

When making vinegar it would be helpful to be able to check alcohol content at various stages, to establish when alcoholic fermentation has completed, and to check for the end point of acetic fermentation without having to rely on extrapolating from acid-base titration data. It can also be helpful to know vinegar alcohol content from religious and addiction recovery perspectives.

Unfortunately, for the home vinegar producer this remains but a dream, with digitised handheld detectors costing about £1,000. A local laboratory will be able to help for approximately £25 per test, but you may have to provide a large sample. There are reagents that can detect the OH group found in alcohols, but all are too dangerous to be used outside a laboratory. This leaves limited options:

- A vinometer, which is a miniature glass tube with a fine nozzle at one end and a chalice at the other. It assesses viscosity, which is greater in beverages with a higher alcohol content, but almost useless to detect low levels.
- Alcohol test strips for saliva can detect up to 0.3 per cent alcohol with colour differentiation, but again, are not reliable for this purpose – I have had problems with false negatives. You'd have to include a control at 0.3 per cent alcohol, and use two strips every time.
- If you were fortunate enough to own a still with a fractionation column (technically it is illegal to operate one without a licence) you could distil some alcohol base, or finished vinegar, collect the distillate and use an alcoholometer to reliably assess the alcohol content of the pure distillate.

Developing Your Own Alcoholometer Scale
Here is a partial solution: during vinegar production, alcohol reduces and acetic acid increases. Acetic acid is denser than alcohol, so the specific gravity will increase on a hydrometer (it will rise again); however, it

is extremely difficult to translate this information into a meaningful figure. The density of acetic acid alters depending on how concentrated it is, and with other complexities – including dissolved sugars, residual alcohol, and sequestration of sugar due to vinegar mother growth – you are fighting a losing battle.

Use an alcoholometer to develop your own relative scale.

What you can do, however, is use a hydrometer or alcoholometer to create a relative scale. Take readings as follows:

- At the end of alcoholic fermentation.
- After the addition of vinegar starter (preferably of known acetic acid concentration).
- Weekly as the oxidative fermentation proceeds (or every three days for rapid methods).
- Every three days (or daily for rapid methods) as the fermentation slows.

- When you have identical consecutive readings, it is likely that you've reached the end point.

Over time, if repeating the same fermentation, you will be able to get a feel for what you are looking for, and might even be able to get a reproducible number on the scale, especially if you are measuring your acidity accurately. From experience, and calibration with acid base titration, I know that when the alcoholometer is at the point shown in the photograph, I am likely to have 5 per cent apple cider vinegar with very little alcohol.

CHAPTER 9

TROUBLESHOOTING THE VINEGAR-MAKING PROCESS

LOW ACIDITY OF FINISHED VINEGAR

It is not uncommon for home-made vinegar to be less acidic than planned, for a variety of reasons. A survey of my own home-made vinegars gave the following results; as you can see they are quite variable. For drinking vinegar, salad dressings, quick-pickling, as long as it tastes good, it's acidic enough. For long-term preserving, flavoured vinegars or cleaning, you will need at least 5 per cent acidity. This can happen for several reasons, as described below.

Evaporation

We have already mentioned that evaporative losses are a perennial problem for vinegar-makers, meaning that less alcohol is available to be fermented to vinegar, and some acetic acid will also be lost. Exacerbated by time, high temperature and high humidity, its management is always a balancing act, because longer cooler fermentation will also result in evaporation. Using a fermentation box to reduce airflow (*see* page 50) or continuous culture (*see* page 83) at room temperature with regular top-ups of alcohol, or step-wise additions, are the least evaporation-sensitive

Type of Vinegar	% Acidity	pH	Age	Method
(w/v acetic acid)				
Apple Cider (1)	5.1	3.3	1 year	Batch
Apple Cider (2)	4.8	3.3	2 months	Batch
Elderflower	4.4	3.5	6 weeks	Boerhaave
White Wine	5.2	2.8	3 weeks	Mini Generator
Scrap Quince	3.2	3.5	3 months	All-in-one
Kombucha	2.2	3.1	1 year	Continuous culture
Mixed	7.1	2.9	6 months	Continuous culture
Beer	3.9	3.3	4 months	Batch
Persimmon	2.5	3.6	2 months	All-in-one

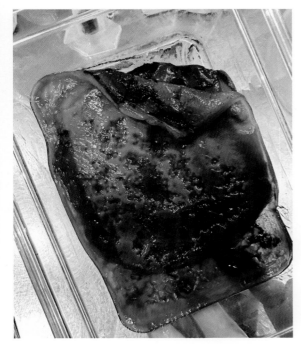

When you forget about a small volume of vinegar – evaporation in action.

methods. If temperatures are very warm, say into the high 30s, it could be wise to place a glass lid or plate over a fermenting vessel, removing daily to allow re-oxygenation to occur. Another strategy is to mitigate against evaporation by increasing alcohol added, which is why 7 per cent is used as a starting concentration throughout the book. This will allow for almost 30 per cent evaporation (which really can happen!) while still resulting in 5 per cent final acidity.

Starting Alcohol Concentration

Sometimes, problems with final acidity can go all the way back to insufficient alcohol in a home-made base. Hydrometer readings are a useful tool but accuracy can be a problem, either with trying to interpret initial sugar levels in thick must, or not having dissolved the sugar fully before testing. This is another reason for aiming for 7 per cent alcohol in the base – it should balance out some inaccuracies.

If it's a recurring problem with a particular type of fruit wine, it might be that some other component

is resulting in false high sugar readings; try and work backwards, and repeat, adding extra sugar to account for the reduced acidity you've seen. For each percentage reduction in acidity add approximately 20g/l and see if that makes a difference to the next batch. Remember to make a note of quantities and hydrometer readings so you can compare results.

Neglect

The vinegar-making process, especially with the slower surface method, can tolerate a good deal of neglect, but if you forget about it completely, you may find your acetic acid yield depleted. When the alcohol source has been used, to avoid starvation the AAB will begin to cannibalise the acetic acid they've made, converting it to water and carbon dioxide.

Stuck Oxidative Fermentation

The yield might be low because the process is not complete. Sometimes strong flavours can mask the presence of alcohol, and as we know this is difficult to test. Also consider the following factors:

- Is the alcohol content of your base within the ideal range? If below 5 per cent or above 9 per cent you could have problems – either dilute it, or add some vodka (or similar) to raise it.
- Are there sulphites in your wine that are inhibiting the AAB? If so, add hydrogen peroxide to remove them (see page 47) and re-inoculate.
- Have you used the correct inoculum of either liquid or solid vinegar mother (see page 26) Less than 10 per cent w/v or v/v can cause problems. Add more starter vinegar.
- Is your vinegar mother viable or has it been skulking in a cupboard at the bottom of a jar for months? Add more, fresh, starter vinegar.
- Are you being patient enough? At cooler temperatures it can take four weeks or even longer for the process to get going. Consider moving your set-up to somewhere warmer.
- What method of production have you used? In all-in-one methods, there will be competition between yeasts, AAB and other microbes for sugar. This will reduce the availability of sugar for

the yeasts to make alcohol from, and ultimately reduce the yield. Add some alcohol to the system, to give a final concentration of an additional 5 per cent per litre (use our $V_1C_1=V_2C_2$ equation to work out how much, see page 55), and a dash of active vinegar mother.

If you would like to increase the acidity of a vinegar that you believe to be completed, this can be done by adding some more alcohol in the form of a neutral flavoured spirit. However, make sure that you dilute the alcohol (see page 55 for calculations), including some fresh mother of vinegar.

Fizzy Vinegar

On opening a bottled live vinegar, occasionally you may hear a pop and see bubbles rising. This is most likely to occur in sweet vinegars and is a sign that either there are active yeasts and sugar still present, or that malolactic fermentation is underway. It is more common in wild ferments, whereupon *Lactobacillus* sp. convert malic acid present in the mix to lactic acid (which can infer a 'buttery' taste). Carbonation can arise either when you are using a mother that has come from a previous all-in-one fermentation, or where acid-tolerant yeasts have become incorporated into the mother, or again were present in a wild all-in-one

There are several reasons for vinegars to be or become fizzy – usually yeast activity or malolactic fermentation.

fermentation. Persistent kahm yeast in a batch could be a warning. You can either:

- Accept that fermentation is not complete and you will have a slightly carbonated vinegar that you will need to vent regularly to avoid a potentially exploding bottle.
- Put the vinegar back in a cloth-covered vessel to allow fermentation to complete. This will reduce the overall sugar content and sweetness of the vinegar.
- If you want to keep the taste exactly as it is, maintaining the sweetness and level of acidity, pasteurise it.

I would recommend checking any wild vinegar batch for such activity 24 hours after bottling.

Vinegar Too Sweet

If the vinegar is too sweet, this is usually the result of using a liqueur or sherry, such as Pedro Ximenez, as a starting base. Lots of sugar in your vinegar will lead to prolific growth of cellulose, so the problem will eventually sort itself out as the microbes convert and thus remove the sugar from the solution you are fermenting. It should not impede the production of acetic acid as the microbes can produce both vinegar and cellulose simultaneously, though you might have to be patient.

Mother not Forming

The presence or absence of a visible mother is not necessarily an indicator of successful vinegar production, as AAB can produce vinegar even if they don't possess the specific genes and cellular machinery to make cellulose. Especially with scrap or wild vinegars, you may find that you have an appreciable acetic acid content after a few weeks with no visible sign of a mother at all.

Second, cellulose production requires a source of sugar and sometimes additional nutrients. A very dry alcohol base might lead to poor growth of visible mother, but vinegar will still form. However, if there is neither mother nor smell nor taste of vinegar, perhaps you have added a non-viable starter. Remove any remaining cellulose and re-inoculate. Low nutrient vinegars, such as spirit-based ones, for example pomegranate vodka, can need a pinch of Marmite or a dash of beer to help them along, in addition to a dessertspoon of sugar per litre.

Third, if you keep disturbing your vinegar to see if a mother has formed, you will significantly delay its progress. Before it is visible to the naked eye, microbes will be at the surface making cellulose and knitting it together. Disturbance will prevent this. If you are aerating your vinegar too vigorously, or using a submerged system, it's not likely that a surface mother will form at all; it will probably be on the air stone.

CONTAMINATION ISSUES

Kahm Yeast

The growth of a pellicle of yeast on the surface of vinegar is a common issue. It arises when yeast is present in the second stage of vinegar production, or in poorly stored finished vinegar. These yeasts are often referred to by the collective term 'kahm'. Yeast can be introduced in several ways:

- In all-in-one fermentations or using home-made fruit or vegetable wines for vinegar production, where acid-tolerant yeasts may still be viable. They will move to the surface and form a pellicle as a way of protecting themselves against the increasing concentration of acetic acid.
- When introducing a vinegar mother (solid or liquid) from a previous home-made batch, which could contain viable wild yeasts, into bought wine or spirits.
- When yeasts in the air colonise a batch of newly forming vinegar, or old, weak vinegar.

Pellicles may exist as a fine film, as though talcum powder has been sprinkled over the top, or as a thick ridged carpet, where the quorum-sensing abilities of microbes will have enabled the development of a detailed pattern. It's difficult to know which yeasts are involved; species such as *Pichia, Debaromyces* and *Zygosaccharomyces* are known to have this capability, as are several species of *Saccharomyces cerevisiae* – in fact, in the caves of Jerez where sherry is made, the surface growth of these yeasts as 'flor' is essential to the ageing process.

The pellicles have different characteristics to the vinegar mother; their waxy nature can prevent oxygen from reaching the brew, thus slowing down vinegar production. Some pellicle formers also utilise alcohol, so potentially could reduce the final acidity of your vinegar, and can produce odd odours – a cheesy, smelly sock flavour being one of them.

Swift removal of a carpet of kahm from the surface is usually sufficient to see it off. This can be done with a spoon, scraping gently to the edge and then up the side of the vessel. If it does regrow, try spraying with 'Magic Spray' or even neat vodka. If this doesn't work, filtering can help.

Kahm yeast microbes seem to be able to grow on all sorts of surfaces – even nutrient-poor vinegars such

Kahm can form in various ways: a) in a poorly stored bottle of raw vinegar, and b) and c) across the surface of new batches.

Flor is an essential part in the ageing process of some sherries, but we don't want it in our vinegar. Wikimedia commons: El Pantera, CC BY-SA 3.0

These fruit flies are fascinating creatures when you see an enlarged image – they love vinegar. Adobe stock

Admire the intricacy of the pattern, then remove it!

as unsupplemented cucumber/vodka vinegar are susceptible. Whilst kahm microbes are not harmful, their long-term presence can create 'off' flavours in the final product. To minimise risk of kahm, use a vinegar mother starter you have purchased from a reputable source, or that you have started from commercial raw ACV, which will be unlikely to contain kahm cultures. Bear in mind, though, that it can still happen through natural colonisation.

Fruit Flies (*Drosophila melanogaster*)

There is no escaping it, fruit flies absolutely love vinegar. From the end of April until November, if you are making vinegar, you will be unavoidably sick of the sight of them! Given any opportunity they will find their way into your brew, so it is important to use a tight-weave cloth or robust kitchen paper cap. In the

A low-cost solution to the problem: use quite potent vinegar and a teaspoon of sugar and they will happily flock to their death.

height of the summer you can make a fruit-fly trap, just like a wasp trap, by inverting the top half of a cut bottle over the bottom half and filling the base with kombucha or vinegar. If fruit flies do find their way into your brew, get them out of there quickly before they lay eggs. Note that they carry AAB on their feet, so they can also add some diversity to your brew! They can also carry other less pleasant microbes, so although most people would just fish them out, there is a theoretical risk of acid-resistant microbial contamination.

Vinegar Eels

Vinegar eels are tiny (2mm) harmless nematodes, but they are a potential contamination issue, especially from orchard fruit. They love this acidic environment and feed on mother of vinegar and/or dead bacterial and yeast proteins. They are a rare enough issue that in fifteen years of vinegar making, I've never seen them. But should you see a throng of tiny worms wriggling in your vinegar, you can either pasteurise and strain the vinegar, or use it to feed some baby fish – vinegar eels are grown deliberately for this purpose.

I have never experienced contaminated vinegar, so I ordered some vinegar eels online just so I could photograph them. I kept this well away from my own cultures, but also realised that they are so tiny, I might not even notice them.

Mould

Mould contamination is unusual; the high acetic acid content and low pH are preventative, even just after inoculation. However, there are a couple of exceptions. First, were you to abandon a jar of vinegar with a mother of vinegar on top, and this grew very thick until all the liquid was evaporated and completely forgotten about, you might find after many months that mould had grown on the top. The mother should be discarded immediately and the jar sterilised before being used again.

Second, if unpasteurised vinegar is stored with a lot of air, microbes will eventually use acetic acid as an energy source (as we've mentioned before), thus raising the pH and reducing the protective quality of the vinegar. In this instance mould could grow at the interface. Always discard anything mouldy or suspect.

INTERESTING SMELLS YOU MAY ENCOUNTER DURING YOUR VINEGAR JOURNEY

It is a harsh but true fact that wild vinegars can have a slightly uriney smell, even though they may taste great. This is most common with wild, slow surface

Virtually invisible to the naked eye unless in enormous quantities, these harmless nematodes could eventually ruin the flavour of your vinegar.

Learning to smell what is going on with your vinegar can give you a mine of information.

processes, and is the result of microbes other than *Sacchromyces cerevisiae* and AAB breaking down nitrogenous compounds in the must. It can be avoided by pasteurisation of must before and/or after making alcohol, or by the use of Campden tablets before fermentation and the addition of commercial yeast. Technically, silica compounds called zeolites can be used to remove these molecules, but I don't really think it is necessary.

A vomity smell is something I hope you never experience from your vinegar. This is the smell of butyric acid (and is what you smell when you are sick):

it is a sign of fermentation gone very wrong, and you should dispose of everything immediately. It cannot be rescued.

A cheesy smell is often associated with the presence of a yeast film on top of your vinegar or wine. This is never very pleasant, but a yeast film that is swiftly removed by scraping off and filtering will have no long-term deleterious effects.

A vinegar smell during alcoholic fermentation simply means that somehow you've managed to get AAB in your wine, and that vinegar production is already underway. However, you might get a lower yield of acidity if the alcohol reaction hasn't finished. During acetification, this is an excellent sign that your vinegar is nearing completion, especially if you can't smell alcohol.

A smell of sauerkraut that isn't as acrid as vinegar could mean that some lactic-acid bacteria have made lactic acid for you. This is most likely in all-in-one vegetable fermentations, which I don't recommend. If something has lactofermented by mistake in the absence of salt, I do not recommend eating it. It should be discarded.

An overwhelming smell of solvent means that the conversion of alcohol to vinegar is going through its intermediate stage, and you can smell acetaldehyde (*see* page 25). This is usually transient but can be the result of stuck fermentation (*see* page 110). It can happen in unvented containers – for example in a vinaigrier with a solid lid. Vent every day to allow oxygen to enter the system.

A solvency yet fruity and delicious smell can be that of ethyl esters, which can also be intermediates in the process, occurring in small quantities as a result of an interaction between acetic acid and alcohol.

If it tastes or smells musty or 'old', it can mean that it has been ready for a while and is beginning to break down the acetic acid. Those odours are breakdown products.

CONTINUOUS CULTURE

Continuous culture is a way of ensuring a constant supply of vinegar. As a starting point, setting it up is exactly the same as setting up a batch surface fermentation, but once up and running, the brew will be consistently active, giving you a constant supply of fresh vinegar, and can be used at any time to seed further batches. You will need a vessel with a tap: 3, 5 or 8ltr dispensers, a vinaigrier or a wooden barrel, and a cloth cover. You can start with alcohol as the base, or even use an all-in-one fruit-juice fermentation.

It builds on the principle of total acidity we touched on earlier, those levels fluctuating between high alcohol, low acidity to low alcohol, high acidity. With a monthly removal of a litre or so, and the addition of a bottle of wine (remember those frozen dregs you can save up), you can end up with a system that can almost constantly supply you with vinegar straight from the tap, save a few days recovery. If you do this weekly, removing 250ml and

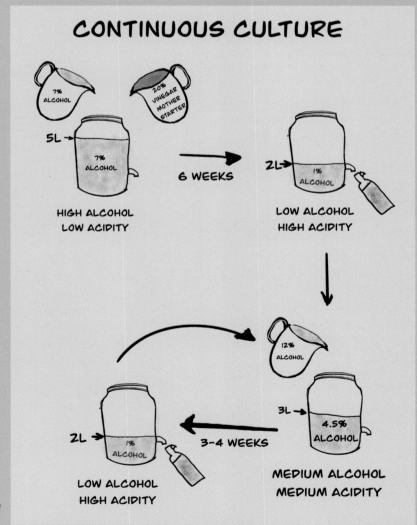

CONTINUOUS CULTURE

7% ALCOHOL

20% VINEGAR MOTHER STARTER

5L →

7% ALCOHOL

6 WEEKS

HIGH ALCOHOL
LOW ACIDITY

2L →

1% ALCOHOL

LOW ALCOHOL
HIGH ACIDITY

12% ALCOHOL

3L →

4.5% ALCOHOL

MEDIUM ALCOHOL
MEDIUM ACIDITY

2L →

1% ALCOHOL

3-4 WEEKS

LOW ALCOHOL
HIGH ACIDITY

Weekly or monthly drawing off and replacing will result in an constant supply of moderately strong vinegar – adding without drawing off will result in a much higher acidity until the limit of the AAB is reached.

topping up with 250ml, you will be surprised that within a couple of days you can't taste alcohol at all.

Mix it up, or keep it single variety, the choice is yours. The diagram illustrates the principle. When you add, for example, 1ltr of 12 per cent wine to the remaining 2ltr of vinegar in the jar, you are adding that to an estimated 1 per cent of alcohol left in the vessel, making 13 per cent. The remaining 2ltr of vinegar in the jar acts as a diluent, so there's no need to dilute your alcohol any more. We will have 3ltr of wine containing 13 per cent alcohol, so that's about 4.3 per cent alcohol per litre – a little lower than the 7 per cent we're always discussing, but that's how this system works. If you don't draw off any, yet top up a little more with some leftover wine, the amount of acid will increase with the stepwise additions of alcohol. Remember to do the following:

- Remove old sunken vinegar mothers.
- Clean the vessel and tap sometimes, or bits of sunken mother can occlude the tap.
- In the summertime, you might need to put a cork in the tap to prevent fruit flies from living in the spout.

Managing Continuous Culture

This method is an effective anti-waste strategy for left-over drinks. In our house it has become a mélange of strange-flavoured beers, left-over wines, with a glass of apple juice and a splash of vodka if it's been left for a while. A mixture of drinks over time will produce a completely unique vinegar, and with regular small additions, a concentrated vinegar can be maintained, which can be drawn off weekly and bottled.

As mentioned, after several successive top-ups, if you don't empty it, the concentration of acetic acid in your vinegar will increase – that is, until the acid tolerance of the AAB is reached. In your weekly checks you will spot this coming, as mother growth will become weaker and patchy. This can also be a sign that nutrients are needed, so add 5 per cent volume of fruit juice or beer to the mix.

This constant addition, and gentle challenging of AAB with alcohol, can lead to potent vinegars – I have had 8 per cent acidity in continuous culture.

You are not likely to be able to make dangerously strong, corrosive vinegar through home production, but undiluted strong vinegars are more likely to cause indigestion/irritation. Check the percentage acidity by titration or with a kit, or at least dilute 50/50 with water when first tasting to get an idea of how strong it is. When bottling, you can dilute to 5 per cent if required, or keep it as it is, noting the concentration on the bottle.

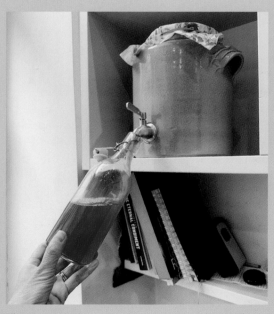

Vinegar on tap.

CHAPTER 10

VINEGAR RECIPES USING READY-MADE ALCOHOLS

The recipes in this chapter are more concepts, or suggestions, than recipes, as the process is the same for each – please *see* page 46 for the flow diagram.

ALEGAR

Alegar – that is, vinegar made from beer – seems to have almost completely disappeared from use by the eighteenth century, and been replaced by malt vinegar, which uses an alcohol base made with malted barley. The component that makes a difference is, of course, hops.

Hops are the flowers of *Humulus lupulus* and one of the four essential ingredients of beer, together with water, malt and yeast. Their presence adds bitterness, and they are important for the foam that sits atop your pint – but they were originally added for preservation reasons. Hops were introduced to England in the late 1400s and have been used ever since.

Chef Alan Coxon understands the value of alegar as a cooking ingredient and has decided to bring it back! He's been working for over ten years on the perfect recipe for his Ale Gar ©, which is currently in production – it is aged for three years in wooden barrels before being bottled.

To make a successful alegar requires a good strong ale, with more than 7 per cent alcohol; after adding

Ale-Gar with oysters, by chef Alan Coxon. Alan Coxon

about 20 per cent active starter vinegar, this will dilute it down to about 6 per cent – but don't worry, because as already mentioned, you will be adding some acetic acid to compensate. If you have a beer that you are particularly fond of that is not strong enough, you can add some vodka, or another neutral spirit to increase the alcohol concentration. AAB find beer nutritious, so there is no need to add anything else.

PEDRO XIMINEZ VINEGAR

As we will see, the creation of balsamic vinegar is a lengthy process (*see* page 138). I have found a shortcut to create something that approximates the rich caramelly taste, using sweet sherry. A cheap solution it isn't, requiring the sacrifice of at least a half, and maybe even a whole bottle of Pedro Ximinez – but it's worth it!

A last word: know your starter! When vinegarising sweet wines that are high in sugar, it can be helpful to avoid the addition of wild yeasts and *Lactobacillus* sp., which might still be viable within wild fruit vinegar mothers. This could result in continued fermentation after bottling, giving you fizzy vinegar.

Sherry vinegars grow prolific cellulose – within a few days they will cover the entire surface and be a clearly visible couple of millimetres thick – but don't be fooled: it will take a lot longer for the vinegar to develop its flavour. No additional nutrients are usually necessary.

I advise not to make less than a litre of this; I tried with less and ended up with 100 per cent evaporation, leaving a mere smear of tangy syrup behind.

FLAVOURED SPIRIT VINEGARS

Given that pure spirit vinegar is the very cheapest type of vinegar – at the time of printing about 70p per litre – there's little point in making your own pure spirit vinegar unless you have a still (and here in the UK you need a licence for that). You won't be able to beat the price, as it's rather costly to buy a bottle of vodka, and plain vinegars don't taste very special.

However, with the addition of botanicals and juices, spirit vinegars can undergo acetic fermentation to make sharp, delicious products with the ability to preserve and enhance some of the flavours. A cherry wine, for example, may taste delicious, but it won't necessarily taste of cherries. With a cherry vodka vinegar, however, there will be no doubting its origins.

A little extra help can be needed for the AAB here, especially if the flavours you are adding aren't nutrient dense: these can be provided in the form of yeast extract, yeast nutrients, or a splash of apple juice, or even beer. Add a tablespoon per litre of sugar to help with cellulose mother growth.

Spirit-based vinegars are best quickly fermented at warmer temperatures. I would recommend the Boerhaave method or a mini generator set-up, as nutrient-poor vinegars don't do so well with the surface method.

Limoncello/Arancello vinegar

If you get into the habit of peeling and freezing the zest from lemons and oranges before you use them in recipes (it's easier than trying to remove from spent citrus), you will be able to amass a sizeable hoard that can be transformed not only into scrap vinegar (*see* page 130), or limon- or arancello, but also a delicious citrussy spirit-based vinegar. Any citrus peel can be used – grapefruit, bergamot, lime, clementines. I

Shave the skins off with a serrated peeler, leaving as much bitter pith behind as possible.

recommend shaving off just the peel with a serrated peeler, leaving as much bitter pith behind as possible.

Use a bland vodka, or a flavoursome gin – either will result in a beautiful clear vinegar that is as delicious for dressings as it is for an aperitif with sparkling water.

The first stage of this process is to make limon- or arancello.

Ingredients

Citrus peels from three or four large lemons
175ml vodka (or similar bland alcohol, approximately 35 per cent)
1tbsp sugar
Yeast nutrient or Marmite
200ml active vinegar starter
625ml water

Method

- Steep the peel in the spirit in a lidded jar for two to three weeks, shaking it when you pass just to help it along.
- Strain the peels from the vodka and discard them. At this point you could always change your mind and stick with limoncello, adding a little icing sugar dissolved in a teaspoon of water for sweetness, and pop it in the freezer.
- This can be diluted to make about a litre of vinegar – proceed to your chosen acetification method instructions, adding in the nutrient and sugar.

POMEGRANATE VINEGAR

This is another delicious and vibrant vinegar that is easy to make – use gin, vodka or tequila here for delicious results. Fruit-infused spirit vinegars are good for fruits with a lot of flavour, and which are quite costly to buy in bulk. Passionfruit also works well (use two or three in the same volume), cherries and hibiscus flowers (add three or four tablespoons).

Ingredients

1 pomegranate
175ml vodka (or similar bland alcohol, approximately 35 per cent)
1 tbsp sugar
Dab of yeast nutrient or Marmite

Pomegranate seeds steeping in vodka.

200ml active vinegar starter
625ml water

Method

- Steep the pomegranate seeds in the spirit in a lidded jar for two to three weeks, shaking daily.
- Strain the seeds from the vodka. They can be sprinkled on some yoghurt – they will still taste of pomegranate.
- Mix the remaining ingredients together and proceed to your chosen acetification method instructions, adding in the nutrient and sugar.

CUCUMBER VINEGAR

Cucumber vinegar is based on first extracting the 'essence of cucumber' using a cheong, a Korean sugar syrup in which a substance is mixed with its weight in sugar and left for some weeks. Due to osmotic pressure, the plant cells yield their moisture, further dissolving the sugar, which creates a syrup. Almost any fruit and many vegetables can be treated in this way – particular favourites of mine are strawberry, raspberry, passionfruit and blackcurrant.

The cheong is added to the diluted spirit at a ratio of 20 per cent. The resulting vinegar is tangy and sweet, with the unmistakable aroma and taste of cucumber – excellent for dressing salads, and for diluting as a drinking vinegar. The syrup provides sugar for mother of vinegar growth, though a pinch of nutrient (yeast nutrient, Marmite, a splash of beer) would be helpful here as cucumber is not nutrient dense – you won't taste it in the final product.

Ingredients needed (for 1ltr)

For the cheong:
100g cucumber, grated, seeds removed (they can be bitter)
100g white sugar
For the vinegar:
175ml alcohol (40 per cent approximately)
75ml cheong
200ml starter
550ml water
Pinch of yeast nutrient

Method

- Steep the cucumber in the sugar for at least one week.
- Strain out the cucumber (it's a weirdly delicious, sweet cucumber).
- Make up the quantities as shown above.
- *See* the universal instructions on page 46.

Vodka-based vinegars: cucumber keeps its flavour beautifully yet is more complex than infused versions.

CHAPTER 11

PREPARING ALCOHOL BASES FOR YOUR VINEGARS

If you haven't made alcoholic beverages before, rest assured that you don't need to be a master wine maker or brewer: this is a forgiving process, and even quite 'unusual'-tasting home-made wines can make complex, delicious vinegars. Making your own bases gives you ownership over the entire process: you will be able to choose your produce and learn a whole additional set of skills. These are low-alcohol bases as opposed to fine wines or award-winning beers, but there's nothing to stop you from taking this part of the process to the next level, making full-strength wines, saving some for drinking and vinegarising the rest.

PREPARING JUICE OR PULP FOR VINEGAR/WINE MAKING

This section describes general principles that will help you to prepare fruit either for all-in-one fermentation, or for making alcohol bases for two-stage fermentation. We will cover how to check that there is enough sugar to turn into alcohol and subsequently vinegar, and that the pH is at the right level for happy yeasts.

A note about terminology: a 'must' is a fruit or vegetable preparation that is to be fermented into wine. I have also used the terms 'juice' and 'pulp' to explain different preparation methods, but both are musts. An alcohol base is a source of alcohol that will be acetified to make vinegar.

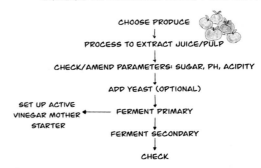

STAGES IN ALCOHOL BASE PRODUCTION

CHOOSE PRODUCE
↓
PROCESS TO EXTRACT JUICE/PULP
↓
CHECK/AMEND PARAMETERS: SUGAR, PH, ACIDITY
↓
ADD YEAST (OPTIONAL)
↓
SET UP ACTIVE VINEGAR MOTHER STARTER ← FERMENT PRIMARY
↓
FERMENT SECONDARY
↓
CHECK

Note that the recipes here are for low alcohol wines to make immediate vinegar bases as opposed to fine wines, but they can easily be increased in sugar content and nutrients to make stronger alcohols that can be aged and/or diluted to make vinegar.

Choosing Produce

There is an extensive list of produce that can be used to make alcohol, including just about every fruit and vegetable, grains, fruit scraps and allotment gluts. I once read that 'the more distantly related the produce is from a grape, the more difficult it will be to make into wine'. I think this is true! If you are fermenting celery, cucumbers or beans you will need to try much harder, so bear this in mind when choosing your resources.

Fresh fruit is usually a reliable natural source of the yeasts and AAB needed for the process as they are important components of their microbiotas, living on the skin and even in the flesh and seeds. Vegetables tend to have fewer yeasts associated with them, so for these wines you may need to add additional yeast if there is no sign of fermentation after three or four days.

Sprouted or malted grains can be a great place to start to make beers, or you can use sprouted rice to make a rice wine starter. The sprouting or malting has activated them, making them rich in sugars for fermentation. We won't be covering beer-making, because that's a whole other process, but we will investigate using saccharification to release sugars from starchy sources (see page 122).

Organic or Non-Organic?

Researchers have found significant differences in the microbial flora associated with organic versus inorganic fruits, both in quantity and type.[21] The significance of these differences has not yet been established, but it is an indication that the use of herbicides and pesticides on our food is not without consequence. The expense of organic produce can be a barrier, with prices often four times that of non-organic, especially when to make a litre of juice you'll need about 2kg of fruit.

The Quality of Vegetables

As the vinegar-making process is a long one, it would be a shame to compromise results by using poor quality produce. Ripe, flavoursome fruit or the freshest vegetables are key to success. This is especially true if you're planning to make the most of the wild microbes for your fermentations, as their populations can decrease with age. Make friends with a local greengrocer: their produce may well be fresher than the shiny supermarket versions, and of more local provenance.

The use of windfalls for making vinegar is possible, but remember they will have encountered all sorts of creatures, and should be properly washed, with bruised areas and cores removed. You may have heard of the toxin patulin, which can be found in mouldy apples. Fortunately it is destroyed by the alcoholic fermentation process, so from this perspective windfall cider and vinegar are both safe to consume.[22]

This one has gone a bit too far! Look at the visible colonies of yeast that have grown.

Look for seasonal, locally grown apples, pears, plums, quinces, garden grapes – often people are crying out for someone to take apples off their hands in the autumn – check on community apps such as Olio or Nextdoor. Alternatively, why not forage for blackberries or bullaces? That way, they are likely to be pesticide free – and probably also free!

Tasting your Produce

While a final vinegar is generally quite forgiving as regards flavour, it is always a good idea to taste your produce first. Sourness isn't an issue, but bitterness is hard to disguise, so cucumbers or courgettes that can be prone to this would not be suitable. Tasteless beets or bland pears are also a waste of time. You will still get vinegar but it won't have the depth of flavour you'll be expecting.

Yield

For apples, pears, stone fruits and juicy vegetables such as beets you can expect a yield of around 50 per cent juice for the weight of fruit. So if you juice 4kg of apples, you will generate about 2ltr of juice. This is one of many aspects of vinegar making that is hard to predict, as the type, specific cultivar, ripeness and age of the produce can all affect this figure.

Using Ready-Prepared Fruit Juice

If you want to skip a stage you can use ready-prepared fruit juice, but be mindful that the results are dependent upon its quality. Heavily processed juices are the least successful; most, even if they state that they are 100 per cent pure, will have been pasteurised or filtered and will have gone through several processing steps. The addition of yeast is almost certainly going to be required to make a wine. If you want freshly squeezed juice, I suggest going to your local friendly juice bar and buying a couple of litres – this is also a great way of getting some interesting combinations.

You can also use frozen fruit, which can be an economical option – mixed fruits are usually better value and can form the base for delicious, rich-tasting berry vinegars.

BATCH SIZE AND EQUIPMENT

Batch size is entirely up to you, as these reactions are scalable. I would recommend the smallest workable quantity to be 1ltr. 5ltr buckets are easily manageable, or you could head towards using 10ltr buckets and 8ltr demijohns.

If you're making a sizeable batch, produce preparation will require some planning. Expect to spend at least one hour to make 10ltr of apple or pear juice, and longer for harder fruits such as quince. For

You will need some help!

Processing big batches will take some time and organisation.

batches larger than 5ltr it is useful to have some help – even if it is just to lift an 8ltr demijohn. Recruit friends and family if you can, and any electric or hand-press juicers they might have.

There's no doubt it will be useful to have something electrical to help you. Juicers are very handy. They do tend to have a cut-out after about 30 minutes of continuous use to protect the motor. There are different types: centrifugal juicers are faster and more affordable, but their juice is said to contain fewer nutrients than macerating juicers.

Most models require a receptacle to collect the juice, which needs to be in place before you start (I write from experience). If you are blending instead, a food processor or work-top blender can do the job; multiple

For larger apples, pears and quinces, a press would be useful. WIKIMEDIA COMMONS ANNE DIRKSE

Simply squeezing grated apple is great for small volumes.

fermentation makes for easy removal – simply lift out the bag and wait for it to drain, giving it a squeeze to help it along. If you can't get hold of one, a colander, sieve and straining spoons are suitable, if messier, substitutions.

small quantities are much better than overloading the machine and will save you time in the long run. If you don't have any electrical machines to help you, think of the most effective way to increase the surface area. This might be grating the produce in question – apples do grate very well, and can be bundled up and squeezed in a muslin cloth or straining bag. You'll be surprised at how much juice comes out.

At the other end of the scale for much larger volumes, garden chipping machines and professional-grade apple crushers would be useful, if you happen to know a friendly cider maker. Or you can stomp your grapes with your feet or wellies if you feel so inclined!

Straining bags are extremely useful and nowadays can even be found in most supermarket produce sections. Placing fruit or vegetable pulp in a straining bag before putting it into a bucket for primary

Juice in a straining bag.

Sterilise all equipment with Campden tablets or one of the other methods mentioned (*see* page 41). Clearly your fruit isn't sterile, but there is no point risking contamination by something festering in your kit from last time.

FRUIT PREPARATION STAGES

Do make sure your fruits and vegetables are clean; if you have just dug up some beets from the allotment there will be a lot of mud, which is not a tasty addition. Orchard fruits can be covered with bird droppings and might have worms and larvae growing within. Some people worry that washing the fruit will wash off all the wild yeasts; this is unlikely as washing is a very ineffective method of sterilisation, but if this is a concern you can wipe your apples clean with a cloth, and leave them for a couple of days at room temperature to build up a healthy yeast population.

Having chosen the produce, you will need to decide how to prepare it – will it be juiced, or mashed up? Methods are dictated by the equipment you have to hand and the fruit type. The general idea is to increase the surface area, facilitating access to carbohydrates for the yeast.

Juicing
Where possible, I prefer to juice fruit and separate the pomace straightaway because I find it less messy, as opposed to fermenting the solids and then having to filter them out later. It is easier to take more accurate measurements in juice rather than in pulp. Juice is less likely to go mouldy because there are no fruit solids, which inevitably float to the top and are exposed to the air.

You may find that a lot of foam is generated. This is caused by saponins in the fruit,[23] and is particularly noticeable with apples and rhubarb; sometimes it sits 5 to 8cm deep. I would recommend reducing this before fermenting. If left, some of it will eventually reabsorb but this can take days, and it may be with you for the duration, serving only as a surface on which mould might settle.

STAGES IN THE PREPARATION OF PRODUCE

HARVESTING
↓
INSPECTING (CREATURES AND DAMAGE)
↓
WASHING (BIRD DROPPINGS/CREATURES)
↓
CUTTING OUT DAMAGED FLESH
↓
REMOVING PITS/PIPS
↓
CUTTING TO CORRECT SIZE FOR MACHINE FUNNEL
↓
ALLOW TIME FOR JUICER TO REST (MOTOR CUT-OUT)
↓
DECANT IN PRIMARY FERMENTATION VESSEL

The main steps in fruit preparation.

Making sure the bowl is firmly in place to collect the juice!

After juicing, wash or dishwash the parts of your machine right away. Don't be tempted to 'leave them 'til later', as sticky fruit residues are much easier to remove immediately.

The variety-specific presence of saponins in fruit can lead to enormous foam production. You may choose to reduce this before fermentation (note that this was placed directly into secondary fermentation). Although it sounds arduous, grating and squeezing through a mash bag is a fantastically efficient way of juicing a smaller volume of apples (*see* page 92).

Juice and Pomace

A good idea is to juice, and then add the pomace back into the juice for maximum extraction of nutrients during fermentation. After juicing, put the resulting pomace in a straining bag and drape it over the edge of the bucket during primary fermentation. It's easier with larger volumes, but it does work with small ones too.

This is the formula for the most nutrient-rich alcohol bases. After this stage, the pulp in the bag can be easily removed.

Fruit Pulp

Others prefer to ferment blended or mashed fruit rather than juice, which can be prepared using a blender or a grater. I would recommend against going too fine – the texture in the first picture on the next page is preferable to the last in terms of ease of processing.

Make sure that you remove pits before blending – you don't want any amygdalin in there from cherry pits as your body can convert it to cyanide! Although apple and pear pips also contain amygdalin these quantities are tiny and not an issue.

You will usually need to add some liquid to the mixture unless the produce is very juicy (ripe, thawed berries for example). If you are concerned about diluting the flavour, adding up to one-third volume is usually compensated for by the nutrients derived from the pulp during fermentation, or you can add pre-prepared fruit juice. Blend the liquid into the fruit well, to enable accurate sugar and pH readings.

Fruit pulps require more attention than juices in the first stages; that top layer of solid matter does need to be stirred daily to stop mould forming and to circulate nutrients, including those released by dead yeast cells. If you forget for even 48 hours you could have a nasty surprise! Pulps also require filtering before secondary fermentation, which can be time-consuming with large quantities. There are a couple of ways to go about this:

- Use a straining bag – this is most definitely the best option.
- Use a slotted spoon if the matter is still on the top in large pieces.
- Hang a large muslin cloth over a bucket to allow filtering (this could take 24 hours for large quantities).
- For small volumes, a sieve will suffice. For larger volumes use a sequentially smaller-sized

The various stages in preparing apple pulp – interestingly, the coarser pulp is far easier to manage and will yield plenty of juice, compared with a fine mash that is quite hard to separate out.

Comparison of juice and pulp extraction methods: which will work best for you?

Juice	Juice & pomace	Pulp
Juicer required	Juicer required	Blender, grater, other mechanical methods possible
Could lose nutrients from pomace.	Nutrient richest	Nutrient rich
No water needed	No water needed	Water could dilute flavour but tends to balance out during fermentation as the pomace yields additional products. You could add fruit juice to mitigate
Less messy	Filtering needed after fermentation	Filtering needed after fermentation
Pectinase not usually needed	Pectinase enzyme may be needed	Can make a hazy product – pectinase can help
Easy to take readings	Easy to take readings of juice fraction	Harder to take accurate hydrometer readings – needs filtering
No stirring needed	Needs stirring to distribute pulp	Needs stirring to distribute pulp

colander/sieve system. You could start with a colander with vertical gaps or large holes, then use a sieve with a wide mesh, then a fine meshed sieve or straining bag. More debris will settle out during secondary fermentation.

Pulps can also require the addition of pectinase, an enzyme that can break down pectin, to avoid a hazy product. If, like me, you are not concerned about clarity in your vinegar, you don't need to add this unless your pulp contains so much pectin that it actually sets (this has never happened to me, but it could).

OPTIMISING THE MUST

While not essential, optimising conditions for alcohol fermentation will lead to more reliable results; here

we will cover the importance of sugar content, pH, nutrition, choice of yeast and temperature.

The Importance of Sugar Content

Unless you are using wine grapes, there is a strong chance the produce will not have a high enough sugar content to make enough alcohol to result in a vinegar with good acidity. Sweet, ripe fruits are more likely to contain ample sugar, while under-ripe fruits, vegetables and grains, scraps and peelings, not so much. There are differences in the natural sugar levels of fruits and vegetables, even within different cultivars of the same species, so it's hard to provide a reliable guide, but here are some useful yardsticks: produce can contain a mixture of sugars that yeast can break down, including sucrose, glucose, fructose and maltose, which are measured in aggregate.

Fruit / Vegetable	Approximate Sugar Content % (g/100g)
Cooking apples	9%
Sweet apples	12%
Pears	10%
Pineapple	10%
Persimmon	13%
Beetroot	9%
Mango	14%
Rhubarb	1%
Tomatoes	3%
Bananas	12%
Peaches	8%
Carrots	5%
Baked sweet potato	12%
Amazake made with rice	23%
Actual wine grapes	18-25%
Bristol garden grapes	7%

Here are some of the sugar levels for fruits and vegetables mentioned in the book. This shows that almost all of them would need some sugar added to make wine, while some won't need any added for alcohol bases for vinegar.

Increasing the Sugar Content

The cherry example in the figure below shows that sometimes produce won't have enough sugar to ensure that your vinegar will meet the 5 per cent acidity zenith. But no matter, there are ways around this, as described below.

Enrichment (Chaptalisation)

Enrichment involves adding sugar to a must to raise the potential alcohol content. In fact there is a school of thought that believes it is a good idea to make a base of a higher alcohol content than you need, and then to dilute it. This can provide more alcohol to act as a solvent for nutrients in the must, and to prevent contamination and oxidation if storing. Elderflower champagne is a case in point – an annual treat not to be missed, some can be diluted to make vinegar, the rest stored.

A slight issue can arise when enriching wild mashes: the extra sugar can feed all microbes present, not just wild yeast, and could allow unfavourable species to flourish. In this case it is wise to add commercial yeast, which will outgrow any competition and ensure a successful fermentation.

CHERRIES NUTRITION FACTS

Total Carbohydrate 12 g	4%	
Dietary fiber 1.6 g	6%	
Sugar 8 g		

If you're making an alcohol base from something not on the list in the previous figure, type, for example, 'cherries nutrition facts' into your search engine, and a generic table will often appear (with a source for the information – this was USDA) for nutrition per 100g: the sugar content is the important factor, as this is what the yeasts can ferment. Cherries contain about 8g sugar per 100g. This translates to 8 per cent sugar, which will be fermented to give about 4 per cent alcohol, which in my experience will produce, again very roughly, 2.5 per cent vinegar.

Concentrating the Must

An alternative enrichment method is to gently heat the must to reduce water content and thus increase the sugar content. A temperature of 70–80°C is recommended, but do be prepared for some change to the flavour from the heating process – in most cases, the cooked versions are less flavoursome as vinegars than their raw counterparts. This is akin to pasteurisation (see page 64).

Saccharification

Saccharification is an additional step that can be used to increase the sugar content of starchy substrates such as grains, rice, pulses or root vegetables. They do contain glucose, but it is locked up in long chains within the starch. During saccharification, amylase enzymes break down starch molecules, which cannot be metabolised by yeast, into their constituent maltose or glucose molecules, which can. You can purchase amylase enzymes directly, but using them is quite fiddly, with a great deal of temperature control required. I favour another method, using rice koji – enzymatically activated rice that we will talk about in our rice vinegar recipe (see page 122). Saccharification is also part of the malting process used to prepare barley for brewing (which I would recommend buying ready prepared from brewing shops) and malt vinegar.

HOW MUCH SUGAR IS REQUIRED?

It's hard to be precise about how much sugar is required. If we look back to our equation (see page 25), to make 1 per cent alcohol you need 19.8g of sugar. But in real life, the amount needed will depend upon several factors: the type of microbes present, sugar type, temperature, the evaporation of alcohol, acidity, the level of nutrients, primary fermentation depletion, and so on. And then there are calculation errors: specific gravity and Brix scales are both affected by other dissolved solids in fruit juices.

This has generated so much debate over the centuries that various 'standards' have been developed,

Predicted Alcohol Concentration	Amount of Sugar *European standard* (g/ltr)	Amount of Sugar *Brix Scale*	Amount of Sugar Used in this Book (g/ltr)
1%	16.83	18	20
2%	33.66	36	40
3%	50.49	54	60
4%	67.32	72	80
5%	84.15	90	100
6%	100.98	108	120
7%	117.81	126	140
8%	134.64	144	160
9%	151.47	162	180
10%	168.3	180	200
11%	185.13	198	220
12%	201.96	216	240
13%	218.79	234	260
14%	235.62	252	280

This table shows the range of the least and the greatest amounts of sugar to add, depending on who you listen to! Full hydrometer and Brix scales are on page 99.

ranging from Adolf Brix's 18g sugar for each 1 per cent of alcohol required, to 16.83g, which is commonly used by wine labs throughout Europe. I am going to suggest 20g per degree of alcohol, which is easy to measure and a suitable standard for home brewing. In any case most of our scales or monitoring devices aren't that accurate.

Note: To make a 7 per cent alcohol base, according to the table above, will require a SG (specific gravity) of approximately 1.060 or 15°Brix, which equates to 7 × 20g (approximately). This table is a guide for adding sugar, which you can then measure with a hydrometer.

Testing with a Hydrometer

Testing the specific gravity (SG) of a must will show how much sugar it contains; this is critical for producing the correct amount of alcohol from yeast fermentation. Testing throughout the process will enable you to find the endpoint, or to work out whether it's got stuck (*see* page 110). If you are starting with a pre-made alcohol base you won't need to use one.

It is said that Archimedes proclaimed 'Eureka! Eureka!', leaping out of his bath and running naked down the street, having noticed that when he got into the bath, the water level rose, whereupon he suddenly understood that the volume of water displaced must be equal to the volume of the part of his body he had submerged. From a 1575 wood carving. HISTORIA NO. 767 – NOVEMBRE 10, PAGE 38

This ingenious and ancient device was invented by Archimedes (300BC). It works using the concept of buoyancy – that things float more or less easily in different solutions: for example, swimming in the Dead Sea is easier than swimming in a lake because the sea is very salty, which makes the water denser. The same applies to sugar: the more of it there is in a must, the denser it will be, and the tube will float. Solutions that contain no sugar and some alcohol are lighter than water after fermentation, and the tube will sink.

Using the Hydrometer

A hydrometer comprises a sealed glass tube, with a wider weighted bottom for stability. There is a specific gravity (SG) scale marked on the stem, which is calibrated at SG 0.000 for distilled water. Modern hydrometers are usually marked with multiple scales, for specific gravity, potential alcohol, and approximate sugar content.

Hydrometers are standardised to be accurate at 20°C, so make sure that your test solution is at room temperature. Even though fruits contain various sugars with different densities hydrometers are standardised

You can buy a hydrometer with not just specific gravity marking, but also a scale to show how much sugar to add and the potential alcohol level.

Specific Gravity (SG) at 20°C	Sugar (g/L)	Potential alcohol %	°Brix
1	0	0	0
1.005	13	0.6	2.7
1.01	26	1.3	3.8
1.015	39	1.9	4.9
1.02	52	2.6	6
1.025	64	3.2	7.1
1.03	78	3.9	8.2
1.035	91	4.5	9.3
1.04	104	5.2	10.4
1.045	117	5.8	11.5
1.05	130	6.4	12.6
1.055	143	7.1	13.7
1.06	157	7.7	14.8
1.065	169	8.4	15.9
1.07	183	9	17
1.075	195	9.7	18.1
1.08	209	10.3	19.2
1.085	222	11	20.3
1.09	235	11.6	21.4
1.095	248	12.3	22.5
1.1	261	12.9	23.6
1.105	275	13.5	24.7
1.11	288	14.2	25.8
1.115	301	14.8	26.9
1.12	314	15.5	28
1.125	328	16.8	29.1
1.13	341	16.8	30.2
1.135	355	17.4	31.3
1.14	368	18.1	32.4
1.145	381	18.7	33.5
1.15	394	19.3	34.6

Use these calculations to guide you, if you don't have alcohol conversion figures on your hydrometer or refractometer. For alcohol stocks we are aiming for about 7 per cent alcohol, Brix 13.5–15, SG 1.055–1.06.

for sucrose. This level of accuracy is perfect for our needs.

Making wine without a hydrometer has been described as 'driving at night without headlamps' – it can be done, but why risk an unsatisfactory result, or potentially waste all the produce you have prepared? Hydrometers are inexpensive (around £10 at the time of publishing), fun and easy to use and worth every penny. Be sure to select one that is for wine making, as versions also exist that are marked up for testing milk, salt water and alcohol.

Equipment needed

A hydrometer, preferably with multiple scales on the side, or use the conversion table (*see* page 99).

A measuring cylinder the same height as the hydrometer – glass will make reading the result easier, plastic will last longer as it's not breakable.

A wine thief, turkey baster or pipette for sampling.

Method

- Ensure all equipment has been sterilised, especially the wine thief (or similar) – it is less important for the other items if you are going to discard the sample after testing.
- Fill the measuring cylinder to about 80ml with must.
- Drop the hydrometer into the cylinder.
- Wait for it to settle.
- Take the reading at the meniscus.
- Readings are not intuitive because only the last two digits on the scale are usually printed, so .65 would mean SG 1.065.

When you have made the must, take a reading with your hydrometer and use it to calculate the sugar content. If it is not within the range, weigh out the appropriate amount of sugar and mix it in well until dissolved. It is best to err on the side of caution as it is easier to add more sugar than remove some. Take another reading to check the level, and record. If it is too high, don't worry – if too much alcohol is produced this can be amended by dilution before the vinegar fermentation stage.

Refractometry

Refractometry is an alternative method for determining the sugar content. When light travels through a liquid it bends, or refracts, and the degree to which this happens can be increased by dissolved components, such as sugar.

This can be measured with a device called a refractometer. It looks rather like a telescope. A couple of drops of must is placed on a glass panel and a plastic cover gently lowered to expel air bubbles. By holding the device up to the light and looking into the eyepiece, a blue scale on a white background will reveal the result. These use the Brix scale, as opposed to the hydrometer's SG, which is standardised to 0° Brix with distilled water. A reading of 15° Brix corresponds to 15g of sugar present in 100g of aqueous solution, so it can also be written as 15 per cent.

So, refractometry or hydrometry: which should you choose? They measure different parameters that both reveal the same information: how much sugar is present. Mostly it is down to personal preference. Hydrometers are cheaper, refractometers require only a drop or two of liquid; hydrometers can be difficult to interpret, refractometers require regular calibrating; hydrometers tend to have a wider range: it's six of one and half a dozen of the other. I would say that

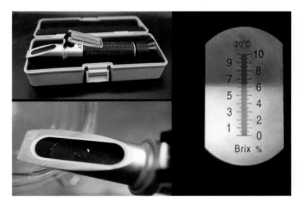

A refractometer looks like a telescope but measures refractive index differences. Place one or two drops on the glass panel, and lower the attached cover gently to expel air bubbles. This is what you will see in the view window, only the line will probably be clearer – it was hard to photograph. This shows 6° Brix.

USING A HYDROMETER

A hydrometer measures the specific gravity of liquids, a parameter that changes when sugar is present. This and a pH meter are the most valuable pieces of kit for a home vinegar maker.

I am making beetroot vinegar. I juice the beets and then take a specific gravity (SG) reading of the juice.

It reads 1.035. Looking at the hydrometer table (*see* page 99) I see that this corresponds to 91g/ltr of sugar and a potential alcohol level of 4.5 per cent. However, this isn't going to be enough for my 5 per cent vinegar.

Consulting the tables again, I can see that a 7.7 per cent alcohol level corresponds to a starting specific gravity of 1.060, requiring a starting sugar concentration of 157g/ltr.

I already have 91g/ltr, so I need to add the difference.

157−91= 66g/ltr of sugar to add.

I add the sugar, stirring well, and once it's dissolved I check the specific gravity again. Of course in this example it's spot on! I write this down, add yeast, and get fermenting.

At the end of fermentation I check again, and see that the SG is 1.000. Anything below 1.004 means that fermentation is almost complete. It might even be a negative number, which happens when fermentation has exhausted every single drop of available sugar, and the amount of alcohol is influencing the reading – alcohol is less dense than water, so makes the hydrometer sink even further.

Close-up of specific gravity of 0.997 and 1.004.

To calculate my final alcohol concentration, I calculate the difference between the starting and finishing readings, and then use a clever formula that has been devised to work out how much alcohol I have made:

(Starting SG – final SG) × 131.25 = percentage alcohol

For our example:

(1.060 – 1.004) x 131.25 = 7.35 per cent (remember the brackets in the order of operations: BODMAS!).

Alternatively, you can plug the numbers into an online calculator.

Note: The magic number, 131.25, comes from an equation that includes the density of ethanol, and how many moles of ethanol and CO_2 are released from the sugar.

---

hydrometers and the SG scale are more commonly used, but refractometers are probably easier. You could start with an inexpensive hydrometer and then later add a refractometer to your toolkit.

Note: If you are using a refractometer to calculate final alcohol level, there is a different formula: (Initial reading – final reading) × 0.55

Hydrometer and Refractometer Readings in Thick/Lumpy Musts

Hydrometers and refractometers work best for liquids. If you want to get a reading from anything thicker with fruit or vegetable pulp you will need a work-around, to avoid inaccurate results. Take a sample of a cupful (250ml) containing both fibre and liquid from the batch, and run it through a blender (you can add it back in, don't worry). Strain out the solids using a sieve and test the strained liquid, using either a refractometer or a hydrometer. Here a refractometer might be better as you don't need much liquid.

If it's still too thick and dry to generate any liquid to test, add some water. Use 100ml water and 100ml of pulp for your sample size. It's a proportional scale so you can double the reading for your result. Blitz together, strain and test the clear filtrate. You can return this to the vessel even though it contains additional water.

Estimating the Sugar Content

If you are a guesser not a measurer, you'll need to estimate the sugar content of the must, approximating

This must is never going to work! You will need to strain this to measure the sugar content accurately. A refractometer will require less liquid than a hydrometer – just a couple of drops.

figures for the produce you are using, and then supplementing, if necessary, according to the table (*see* page 96).

Here's an example: I am making cider using dessert apples. They taste sweet, and looking online they could contain 12 per cent sugar, which equates to 12g per 100g, or 120g per litre.

Consulting the potential alcohol table (*see* page 98), 140g/ltr is recommended to give me 7 per cent, so I should add an extra 20g per litre.

It is important to measure the sugar content, and not just add loads of sugar all in one go, because if you do, the yeast could be completely overwhelmed, its growth inhibited, and fermentation entirely stalled. It's always best to err on the side of caution. To avoid this, if you need to add more than 100g/ltr in one go, consider adding it incrementally, in three portions spread over primary fermentation.

Which Sugar?

So which sugar to use? The most commonly used is refined granulated sugar, but there is no reason why you cannot substitute brown sugars instead – their higher molasses content provides micronutrients that are useful for microbial metabolism. Organic sugar that is not pure white also has a higher mineral content than refined white sugar and is a good compromise, adding nutrients without altering the flavour. The addition of brown sugar will make a difference to the final taste: caramelly, slightly burnt notes will be evident that are not to everyone's taste, but do experiment. Honey can

A variety of sugars can be used in fermentation. SHUTTERSTOCK

be used, but do not use sugar substitutes such as stevia or erythritol as they do not contain any actual sugar, which is essential for alcohol production.

How Much Sugar should be Left at the End of Alcoholic Fermentation?

A specific gravity of 0.997 will indicate that fermentation has exhausted the sugar supply, and this will mean that your alcohol base will be 'dry'. Anything below 1.004 is acceptable – a trace of remaining sugar will help cellulose mother growth and add a little sweetness to a vinegar. If it has gone too far, a teaspoon of sugar per litre can help redress the balance during acetification.

ESTIMATING PH

Many fruits have a slightly acidic pH, which is helpful for alcoholic fermentation in two ways. First, it provides the ideal environment for yeasts to thrive, and second, it can protect against growth of harmful pathogens that could potentially thrive in anaerobic environments – soil pathogens such as *Clostridium botulinum* and some unpleasant *E.coli*. Many vegetables have a neutral or even slightly alkaline pH. The process of yeast fermentation will itself lower the pH, but it can be advisable to acidify vegetable pulps and juices, especially if they are soil harvested.

A pH of 3.5 to 4.5 is optimal for starting fermentation; powdered citric acid, or lemon juice will work. While you could add some of your own vinegar, do remember that some yeasts are killed by quite low concentrations of acetic acid. If you needed to raise the pH, say for extremely acidic under-ripe grapes, you could add some food-grade calcium carbonate – this is available from brewers' shops or online.

During fermentation, the pH will drop a little further; in addition to alcohol, yeast will produce organic acids, and utilise amino acids from the must, reducing the buffering capacity (the ability to soak up hydrogen ions), all of which will lower the pH and increase the acidity. Taking a measurement at the end of the process can also act as a measure of progress. For more information about using a pH meter, *see* page 103.

A pH meter is not essential, but extremely useful to tell you what your vinegar is up to!

pH and Acidity

As we have seen, pH and acidity aren't quite the same. The amount and type of acid present in fruit varies according to variety and cultivar, with an optimal range for fermentation of 5 to 10g/ltr. This can be measured by testing the must with a kit that is available online (made by Biowin), or you can estimate the content by searching online. For our purposes, though, as we are making vinegar not fine wines, I think that pH is a sufficient measure of the acid nature of musts.

Temperature

The best temperature range for most wine yeasts is between 21 and 25°C. If it's too cold your fermentation will slow down and may stop altogether. If it's too warm, the yeast might die off, or in wild fermentations you might play host to less hospitable microbes that can grow at warmer temperatures, resulting in odd flavours, or even spoilage.

USING THE RIGHT MICROBES

Although wild fermentation is often successful, it isn't always the case. Sometimes wild yeasts will produce farmyard-ish odours and/or flavours, and there's no knowing what their tolerance to high alcohol levels might be. There can be problems with attenuation and flocculation, two brewing terms that are discussed below.

If you are looking for batch-to-batch consistency, and almost guaranteed success, consider adding commercial yeast. This is a generic term for yeasts that have been hand-picked for their favourable fermentation characteristics. Although bakers' and brewers' yeasts are both types of *Saccharomyces cerevisiae*, they are different strains and are not interchangeable; bakers' yeast has a low tolerance to alcohol, so it doesn't make very good wine or beer.

Attenuation

Attenuation is a measure of how well a particular yeast strain converts sugars into alcohol, which depends on several factors, including alcohol tolerance. A high attenuating yeast will ferment virtually all available sugar, resulting in a dry finish. A low attenuating yeast will ferment less of the sugar before it runs out of steam, resulting in a sweeter product. Wine and beer makers deliberately choose attenuation characteristics that suit their product, be it a dry cider or a sweet wine. You can check the degree of attenuation in your finished alcohol base using your hydrometer (*see* how on page 101), which can be useful for optimising regularly repeated fermentations.

Attenuation can be affected by the amount of liquid present – the fewer solids in the must, the more likely that sugar will be fermented out. Other factors ensuring that yeast reaches its full potential include the pH range, and nutritional status; healthy yeasts can survive higher alcohol levels.

Flocculation

Flocculation relates to the ability of yeasts to clump together and either rise to the top or fall to the bottom of the vessel. It happens when proteins called flocculins stick out of their cell walls and bind to others. High

High flocculating yeasts easily settle out of the must in clumps, due to the presence of flocculins. This makes them easier to get rid of in terms of clarity, but sometimes can stop them from finishing fermentation completely.

flocculation means that yeasts clump together early in the process; low flocculation means the opposite. Highly flocculating strains can produce a nice clear brew, but sometimes this happens before the fermentation process is complete: yeasts lose access to the sugars in the brew, and fermentation comes to an early end.

There is a bewildering choice of brewer's yeast available; here are some factors to consider when choosing:

- Are you making a fruit or vegetable wine, cider or beer? Yeast strains aren't necessarily interchangeable, with some wine strains making beer taste odd.
- Alcohol tolerance – this can be strain specific. Above 15 per cent alcohol, many will die off. For high alcohol brews you can use sherry yeast, which can tolerate 16 per cent, or turbo yeast, 20 per cent.
- Temperature range: choose according to your circumstances, also being aware that cooler temperatures will deliver slower fermentation.
- Acetic acid tolerance: it's helpful if the yeasts die off during the acetic fermentation stage of the vinegar process, so low tolerance is preferable.
- Low nutrient requirements: fruit and vegetable wines may not have all the nutrients needed for optimal yeast growth.

- Maximum yield: choose high attenuating yeasts to ensure complete or near complete fermentation. Additional sugar can be added before acetic fermentation if required.
- High flocculating yeasts are generally helpful, as this will lead to a clearer end product, despite potential attenuation issues.

For most of your fruit or vegetable wine needs, I'm recommending champagne yeast. This can be a single strain of *S. cerevisiae* or close relative *S. bayanus*, or a mixture of the two. It's a good choice as it can tolerate high alcohol concentrations, low nutrients, and a wide temperature range; it works rapidly, and usually without causing stuck fermentations (*see* page 110).

You may have read about Saison yeast for fruit wines, popularised by Noma restaurant.[24] These are strains of *Saccharomyces cerevisiae* var. *diastaticus* that have historically been used for Belgian beers. They can increase the production of flavour molecules in fruit wines, with high attenuation and low flocculation.

Yeast has a shelf life of about a year, so don't overbuy. Individual sachets are a good idea, as this means that you can change varieties quite often and work out which you like best.

Nutrients

When yeasts reproduce, they need a range of nutrients, including amino acids, nitrogen, fatty acids and vitamins: biotin, pantothenic, acid and thiamine. Although fruit musts might seem to be complex and nutritionally rich substrates, this is not always the case. In early-stage fermentation, yeasts use readily available simple sugars. As these are depleted and the level of alcohol starts to rise, they can struggle unless they are in tip-top condition.

Scrap alcohol bases can be particularly nutrient poor as they are so dilute. Sometimes mixed ingredient mashes will be better sources of nutrients for yeast growth. It is easy to correct with the addition of specific yeast nutrient or diammonium phosphate (DAP): these can be purchased either online or from brewers' shops. Add the recommended amount per litre. If you don't have any to hand, you can use a dab of Marmite, or your own home-made version (*see* below). Usually a gram per litre is recommended.

Tannins also promote healthy yeast growth; powdered tannin is available from a brewer's shop or online, or can be added in the form of loose tea at 0.5tsp/ltr.

Pitching the Yeast

Pitching the yeast is 'brewers' speak' for adding yeast to the must. You should pitch the yeast, or set up your wildly fermenting wine, as soon as possible after juicing to minimise the risk of contamination.

Brewers' yeast comes in sachets or pots, as liquid or dried granules, and should be added in the ratio suggested by the manufacturer – this is usually in the region of 5g per gallon, or 1g per litre, and you might need to guesstimate a pinch, or use some miniature scales for greater accuracy. Sprinkle dried yeast on the top – there's no need to stir, it will gradually rehydrate and sink in, unless you are using a thick pulp – in which case, stir gently.

The yeast will get going faster in temperatures between 20 and 25°C, so ensure that the must is at the correct temperature. Some makers go one step

The yeast will usually melt straight in: there is no need to stir unless the mash is very thick and dry, in which case help it along.

further and activate the yeast first, especially if adding to a wild ferment, to help them triumph over the indigenous microbes (I haven't found this necessary, myself).

For quantities up to 5ltr, simply add the yeast to 250ml boiled water cooled to 30°C in a sanitised jug. Do not stir or it will clump. Cover and leave for 15min. Stir and leave for another few minutes. Pitch within half an hour. Do not expect to see foam as you would with baker's yeast.

PRIMARY AND SECONDARY FERMENTATION

The alcoholic fermentation process can be split into two phases – an aerobic primary followed by an anaerobic secondary one.

Though it is not essential, I would always recommend a spell of primary fermentation for developing yeast health, although other makers feel that the quality of brewers' yeast is sufficient to guarantee good growth, and that aerobic primary fermentation is just a contamination/oxidation risk. They will fit an airlock straightaway.

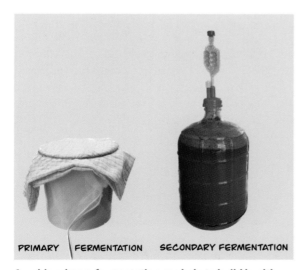

Aerobic primary fermentation can help to build healthy yeast populations, and up to 70 per cent of alcoholic fermentation can occur in this stage. Secondary fermentation, without air, allows the process to complete.

Primary Fermentation

An aerobic stage sounds counter-intuitive, as we have seen that alcohol fermentation is usually an anaerobic process. In Chapter 3, however, we saw that oxygen during the lag phase helps to build healthy yeast cells. It is hypothesised that as dissolved oxygen levels in the must decrease, the yeasts begin fermenting, producing alcohol and CO_2. This is denser than air, and sits above the must in the vessel, effectively creating an anaerobic environment, driving fermentation. It is also possible that the Crabtree Effect (*see* page 22) could be involved, where aerobic alcoholic fermentation can occur with plenty of sugar around – that is, in the early stages of fermentation. It is estimated that as much as 70 per cent of alcoholic fermentation can occur during this stage. Aerobic primary fermentation requires a breathable cover, and the must should be stirred daily for five to seven days, especially if there is solid matter present. Racking the wine between primary and secondary fermentation is recommended (*see* below).

Secondary Fermentation

After five to seven days in primary, the rate of fermentation slows. Wine is usually racked (removed from the lees) and placed in a vessel with an airlock to protect the brew from contamination and oxidation as fermentation slows down. If you are adding an airlock from the start, allow 25 per cent space in your vessel for the volume to increase; CO_2 and froth will be produced in the first stages and could clog the airlock, which could be an explosion risk. If you are primary fermenting, you can fill the vessel almost to the top.

Signs of Fermentation

Whether you engage in primary fermentation or head straight to secondary, frothing will be evident in the first few days of fermentation as the yeast gets going and CO_2 is produced. There will be other visible changes too – the must may split or clear, and if you are using a glass jar you will begin to see lees forming at the bottom of the vessel. When it is visibly inactive, slower, secondary fermentation is underway. Add an airlock if you haven't already, and check the sugar level every few days (*see* page 101).

Signs of fermentation include the presence of bubbles, expansion of the must, and separation into layers with the pulp on top.

For racking you can use a syphon, or a turkey baster for small volumes.

Racking an Alcohol Base

Racking an alcohol base is 'brewers' speak' for removing wine from the lees – the spent yeast cells and debris that sink to the bottom of the fermenting vessel. Prolonged contact with the lees can lead to the development of 'off' flavours, and their removal will help with vinegar clarity. It is carried out between primary and secondary, and when fermentation is complete.

Lees often look as though they are consolidated or compacted, but they usually aren't, and will float up the moment the vessel is tipped, so separation requires various approaches depending on volume. A siphon and pump for decanting into a clean vessel are useful for large quantities – for smaller amounts use a cup measure, turkey baster and some patience. If you have

fermented in a vessel with a tap, if the lees are below tap level, simply open and let it flow. If they aren't you will be better off using a syphon. If you mix it all up by mistake during the process, you can let it resettle and try again. There will come a point when you must leave a little liquid behind.

Ageing Alcohol Bases

Ageing alcohol bases is not recommended if you have made a low alcohol wine; these can be susceptible to spoilage, so start acetic fermentation right away. If you are doing the 'two step' method keep it somewhere cool, or refrigerate, until the second step addition. Higher alcohol wines, above 12 per cent, can be stored for up to a year after racking, for further flavour development. I recommend ageing vinegar instead.

Demijohns in the cool of an understairs cupboard – I recommend ageing wines with an alcohol content of 12 per cent and above.

Pasteurising Alcohol Bases

Pasteurising alcohol bases is not usually necessary. As the alcohol concentration increases, yeasts are normally inhibited and sink to the bottom; in wild fermentations, most microbes will have been outcompeted by the yeast, or will not survive the alcohol. The addition of a recommended 20 per cent vinegar to get acetic fermentation started will usually see off all but the most stubborn surviving yeasts. If you would like to pasteurise, turn to page 63 for the instructions.

Using the Lees

You can make your own yeast nutrient using lees, the debris at the bottom of a vessel after fermentation; lees contain a mixture of dead and dormant yeasts, plant matter, proteins and insoluble salts. This will be most successful with fresher lees.

After decanting the alcohol base, strain the lees through a coffee filter to the stage where it will make thick paste. Hold at 50°C for 24 hours to allow any active enzymes to hydrolyse proteins into amino acids. Spread the resulting paste on to a silicone sheet and dehydrate at 70°C. This temperature will kill any viable yeast. When it has dried, blitz to a powder and store in a labelled jar. This is your own yeast nutrient. It will probably not be as potent as 'bought', so I would recommend half a teaspoon per litre. As Marmite is made from beer lees, if you have made your own beer, you can try this process to make your own! I don't recommend this with fruit-based lees, because the malting process is essential for flavour development.

Batch Size

The volume of alcohol base you are making will have some influence on the speed of the process. In a large volume, it can take time for temperature to equalise – if your juice is cold, this can slow down fermentation considerably. Access of yeast to oxygen in the early days of primary fermentation can also be reduced in a large volume, so do be sure to stir well at the beginning. On the plus side, the effects of evaporation are less noticeable.

Other Additives

Campden Tablets

Campden tablets (named after Chipping Campden, where they were invented) are multi-purpose disinfectants commonly used in wine- and beer-making. They consist of either potassium or sodium metabisulphite, and are added to musts to kill off any unwanted organisms and to inhibit wild yeasts. They are also commonly used as a sanitiser for brewing. While you can use them in making fruit wines, I am not sure that they are entirely necessary for alcohol bases for vinegar making. Even if you aren't planning a wild fermentation, inoculation with brewers' yeast will rapidly out-compete the natural variety and any other microbes hoping to get a look-in. If you are attempting wild acetic fermentation, Campden tablets will prevent that entirely as they are toxic to AAB.

If you do add Campden tablets to a must, let it sit for 24 hours to allow the metabisulphite to do its job, and follow the instructions on the packet.

Pectinase

Pectin is a soluble fibre made of complex carbohydrate chains found in some fruits. We know of it in terms of jam making as it helps jam to set. In making wines and ciders, though, it can cause cloudiness, and sometimes even setting in a must if there's a lot present. The enzyme pectinase can be added to stop the formation of a pectinous mass and subsequent cloudy vinegar. Preparations are available online or in brewing shops, and often also contain cellulase enzymes to expedite the breakdown of your produce. If, like me, you are not concerned about clarity in your vinegar, you don't need to add pectinase. If you want to check the pectin content there is a simple test:

- Place 50ml of methylated spirit in a glass jar with a lid.
- Add 10ml of must (blended).
- Put the lid on and shake for a few seconds.

If a gelatinous mass forms, there is a significant amount of pectin present and you can decide to add pectinase if you wish; if nothing happens, pectin levels are low.

TROUBLESHOOTING ALCOHOL PRODUCTION

Issues are of three types: contamination, which is more likely in wild fermentation situations; interpretation of results; and stuck fermentation, when it just won't work.

Contamination

If you believe something has gone wrong during alcoholic fermentation, firstly use your senses:

- Sight – what does it look like? Mould, excessive cloudiness, distinct colour change could be signs for concern. Is it viscous? In which case lactic-acid bacteria could have produced dextrin.
- Smell – does it smell alcoholic? If it smells like socks or vomit it is likely to be contaminated, or has suffered overgrowth of butyric acid-producing lactic-acid bacteria.
- Taste – only if you have checked the pH and it is below pH 4 should you consider tasting something

Don't forget to stir! H-S-L

hydrometers and refractometers, unless digital, can be subject to error in their interpretation. It's not surprising when you consider that lab equipment for these tests costs thousands of pounds.

Consider a hydrometer: with the tube gently bobbing about at a slight angle in a cloudy apple juice or cider, it is hard to get a clear reading. Also, there's no way of knowing whether other products either in the fruit juice or resulting from fermentation might interfere with results.

Before taking hydrometer readings, check the following:

• that any added sugar is completely dissolved;
• that the sample is at room temperature;
• that the hydrometer can move freely in the sampling vessel – if not, find a wider, taller one.

Stuck Fermentation

'Stuck fermentation' is the term used to describe a situation when the sugar level in the must resolutely refuses to drop when tested with a hydrometer, or no visible signs of fermentation are evident. It can happen in both wild and controlled fermentation, and can simply be to do with the intrinsic attenuating ability of the yeast used.

There are occasions when you may not realise that your fermentation is complete. The process is often thought to be long and slow, but sometimes can be done within three days; you might have missed the signs, and actually it's all over. If your fermentation appears not to have worked, do check the sugar content – you might be surprised to find that your alcohol base is ready.

It can be hard to identify the specific problem – the most likely are listed in the illustration opposite – but in any case most fermentations will get going again with the following triumvirate of actions: a good stir, some added nutrient, and a pinch of commercial yeast.

that could be contaminated. If the pH has risen, something is certainly awry.
• Common sense – did you do anything unusual during the process? Can you check your notebook/spreadsheet?

There is little value in trying to rescue a contaminated batch. Even if you pasteurise and restart fermentation, you wouldn't know whether, for example, heat-stable fungal toxins had been produced. Even though I have myself removed mouldy solids from the top of musts, fungal hyphae will almost certainly grow throughout the entire batch and I am certainly not going to recommend this as a way forward; that's your call.

Inaccurate Hydrometer Readings

Unfortunately, the life of the kitchen scientist is beset with problems; readings taken at home using

Issue	Cause	Solution
Nutrient availability	Lack of required yeast nutrients, most likely in scrap musts, or with unusual produce like beans and courgettes.	Add yeast nutrient and stir well to oxygenate.
Temperature	Most wine yeasts prefer 21-25°C. If it is very cold, then your fermentation will proceed much more slowly. If it is much too warm the yeast may work too fast and deplete nutrients before the sugar has been used up. They can also produce unpleasant estery odours if too warm.	Move must somewhere warmer, or cooler to fit the range. If it's been far too hot, add some nutrient and stir well.
Incorrect sugar	Too much could inhibit yeast growth; too little could lead to starvation and failure to produce enough alcohol.	Hard to assess without a hydrometer; add more if the must is not at all sweet.
Yeast death	Viability of packet yeast is about a year, check the date – they may be past it. If pasteurising must before inoculation, ensure it has been cooled to 25°C before adding the yeast, or you will kill it. If sulphites were added, leave the must for 24 hours, with a loose cover over to give them time to dissipate before inoculation. If your packet yeast requires rehydration, use tepid water.	Re-inoculate with fresh yeast.
Lack of primary fermentation	Some species of yeast benefit from a period of oxygenation to build a healthy population. Unhealthy yeast may become dormant before fermentation can complete.	Aeration and a dash of yeast nutrient can get it going again.
Too much alcohol for the yeast	Wild species especially may not tolerate high levels.	Try aeration with a good stir and adding nutrients. If still no joy after a couple of days, add some commercial yeast.
Early flocculation	High flocculating strains can clump together before fermentation is done.	Stir to break up precipitated yeast.

A summary of the major issues that can occur at this stage, and some solutions.

CHAPTER 12

ALCOHOL BASE RECIPES

In this chapter are some tried and tested recipes for alcohol bases – follow the fruit preparation instructions in the recipe, then use the universal instructions in the figure below.

Note: When you set up an alcohol base, please do remember to get your vinegar mother going at the same time – if it has been dormant for a while it will take two weeks to wake up (*see* page 29)!

GENERAL INSTRUCTIONS FOR ALCOHOL BASES

PROCESS PRODUCE TO EXTRACT JUICE/PULP

↓

CHECK/AMEND SUGAR TO S.G 1.06 OR 15° BRIX

↓

CHECK/AMEND PH TO RANGE 3.5–4.5

↓

ADD YEAST & NUTRIENTS (OPTIONAL UNLESS HEATED)

↓

!!! NOW ALSO SET UP VINEGAR MOTHER STARTER TO GET GOING !!!

↓

FERMENT PRIMARY (AEROBIC) FOR 5–7 DAYS

↓

RACK TO SECONDARY (ANAEROBIC) FOR 7–10 DAYS

↓

CHECK S.G IS 1–1.004 OR BRIX 0–2°

↓

RACK TO ACETIFICATION VESSEL (OR AGE)

General instructions to follow for making alcohol bases. More detail on each point is given in the previous sections.

Let's start with cider for ACV.

APPLE CIDER BASE (AND OTHER ORCHARD FRUITS)

Where better to start than with ACV – your home-made version will be easily as flavoursome as expensive raw commercial versions. There are several different ways to go about this; *see* pages 125 and 130 for simpler, all-in-one and scrap methods.

Choosing Apples

You can use a single variety or a mixture of apples. Dessert apples can have lower levels of pectin and make for clearer vinegars. If you are looking for batch consistency, either go for a single variety, or know the proportions you are mixing – for example 50 per cent Bramleys, 30 per cent Coxes, 20 per cent Russets. You can use authentic cider varieties, which are not edible because of their astringency, but are great for fermenting, if you can find them. Be sure to use ripe apples, otherwise they can contain more starch than sugar, which will be harder for the yeasts to ferment, and will result in too much total acidity.

Make use of the wild microbes that come with the apples, or for reproducibility and control, add

champagne yeast. The wild pot-luck scenario might not seem such a good idea if you're making an enormous batch. I always use juice, but you can use fruit pulp if you choose.

Must from Apple or Quince Juice
Ingredients:

Volume	1ltr	2ltr	5ltr
Apples/quince	2kg	4kg	10kg
Approx. sugar to 1.060 SG	65g	130g	325g

Method:
- Check and wash the fruit.
- Chop to an appropriate size for the juicer funnel (this is optional; remove the cores).
- Juice, remembering to place the collection vessel under the spout first.
- Skim off excessive foam.
- Proceed to general alcohol fermentation instructions, page 112.

Must with Apple Pulp
Ingredients:

Volume	1ltr	2ltr	5ltr
Apples required	1kg	2kg	5kg
Water/ fruit juice	250ml	500ml	1,250ml
Approx. sugar to 1.060 SG/ 15° Brix	65g	130g	325g

Method:
- Check and wash the fruit.
- Place in the blender with the water and whizz until approaching smoothness, but don't overdo it as it will be too fluffy and difficult to manage.
- Proceed to general alcohol fermentation instructions, *see* page 112.

QUINCE CIDER ALCOHOL BASE

Quinces are the most impossibly hard fruit to prepare, and some people choose to cook them in water to soften them before adding yeast and making wine. While this can lead to a vinegar with a beautiful rosy hue, cooking can dull the flavours and personally I prefer to leave them raw. Quinces can be juiced successfully in a heavy-duty machine – if you extract the cores, pips and peels first, keeping them aside for a scrap vinegar, or to enrich the must in a straining bag, the pomace can be used to make membrillo (quince cheese). Quince vinegar is one of my favourites: complex floral and surprisingly sweet. It is suitable for two-stage, all-in-one vinegar or scrap vinegar methods; you can use the same quantities and methods as listed for apple juice above.

PEAR ALCOHOL BASE

Pear cider has its own name, perry, and it is made using very specific cultivars of fruits that are not edible, but make good cider. 'Normal' pears are low in acidity, and the addition of some lemon juice is usually required for a successful fermentation. Some are rather flavourless and you could be disappointed with your final vinegar, so do taste them first. Ripe, juicy Comice are a good choice. Pear scraps will work, but as regards flavour it's best to add them in with apple or quince. Apply the same methods for apple juice with these approximate quantities.

Note: I have recently learned that pears can contain a great deal of sorbitol, which can have a laxative effect, so consuming a moderate quantity as vinegar could be a better idea!

For pear juice:

Volume	1ltr	2ltr	5ltr
Pears	2kg	4kg	10kg
Approx. sugar to 1.060 SG or 15° Brix	55g	110g	275g
Lemon juice	50ml	100ml	250ml

For pear pulp:

Volume	1ltr	2ltr	5ltr
Pears	1kg	2kg	5kg
Approx. sugar to 1.060 SG or 15° Brix	55g	110g	275g
Lemon juice	50ml	100ml	250ml

GARDEN GRAPE ALCOHOL BASE

Grapes from garden vines can make excellent vinegar. They ripen far later than you'd imagine – here in Bristol it can be late October, even early November before they're ready. Ideally they should have a pH of about 3.5 – they

Don't waste that harvest of garden grapes – there will be plenty for both you and the birds to share!

are unlikely to have the sugar content of grapes grown in the Spanish sun, but we can amend this.

Harvest the grapes by snipping with scissors where they join the vine. I wash them, but some makers maintain that this will unnecessarily reduce the yeast population. If the grapes have been sprayed with something or are full of earwigs I recommend it, or you can rest them in a bucket for a couple of hours – most creatures will make a hasty exit. You can buy grapes instead, which should avoid the earwig issue, but not necessarily the pesticides.

Traditionally, white wines are prepared with grapes without the skins, whereas for reds they are crushed and left to ferment with the skins on in primary fermentation, though you can also juice red grapes and make a rosé. Juicing, especially with a good quality machine, will successfully remove the pips without breaking them. Blending is not a good idea here as the pips can add bitter flavours.

Ingredients:

Volume	1ltr	2ltr	5ltr
Garden grapes	1kg	2kg	5kg
Approx. sugar 1.060 SG, or 15° Brix	110g	220g	550g

Method:

- If picking grapes, leave them for a couple of hours on a flat plate, or in a colander over a bucket, to give wildlife a chance to escape.
- Wash if you choose.
- For white wine, use white wine grapes and a juicer to separate skins and pips from the juice.
- For rosé, use red wine grapes and a juicer.
- For red wine – do not separate the skins, but use a potato masher to crush grapes thoroughly, releasing as much juice as possible – you can even use your feet!
- If you are using the skins as well, use a straining bag.
- Proceed to general alcohol fermentation instructions, page 112.

BEETROOT ALCOHOL BASE

Beetroot is a powerhouse of nutrition, full of biologically active phytochemicals, including antioxidants, fibre, polyphenols, minerals and vitamins. When lacto-fermented with salt as beet kvass, these benefits are even more pronounced, with the presence of gut-microbiome-stimulating lactic acid bacteria (LAB). Research[25] has shown that LAB and high antioxidant activity are also present in beetroot vinegar.

Raw beetroot makes a far superior vinegar compared to the cooked version, which tastes dull and lifeless and seems sluggish in acetic fermentation, though I am not sure why. Raw red beet vinegar is rosé coloured with a delicious underlying sweetness, and a slight beetrooty earthiness. You can use golden or Chioggia beets for this recipe, though the colour fades quickly and they contain fewer beneficial polyphenols.

Beets are root vegetables, with a different microflora to tree and bush-grown fruits, including plentiful LAB. They also have a higher pH than most fruits, in the range of 5–6, which is quite high for yeast fermentation, and low acidity. While there may be yeasts present, for guaranteed success add champagne yeast and amend the pH to 3.5–4.5 with lemon juice or citric acid.

Beetroot wine can ferment extremely vigorously. If you miss the endpoint and it ends up overshooting the ideal 1.000 specific gravity level, add a little fruit juice or additional sugar for reliable mother formation when

Beets are such a triumph as a vinegar. Keep this one raw for the best flavour.

it comes to the vinegar stage. Sometimes beetroot wine can be so nutrient dense it can even inhibit AAB. To avoid this, I usually make a weaker must, diluting one-third with water, which seems to help. This can be made either by juicing the beets and diluting with one-third water, or grating or cubing them and mixing one part beet to two parts water.

Ingredients:

Volume	1ltr	2ltr	5ltr
Beetroot for juicing/ water to add	1.5kg/ 300ml	3kg/ 600ml	7.5kg/ 1.5ltr
Grated beetroot steeping (peeled weight)	300g/ 600ml	600g/ 1,200ml	1.5kg/ 3ltr
Approx. sugar 1.060 SG, or 15° Brix	100g	200g	500g
Lemon juice or citric acid to lower pH	50ml	100ml	250ml

Method:
- Thoroughly wash and scrub the beets and choose your preparation method.
- Proceed to general alcohol fermentation instructions, page 112.

BLACKBERRY ALCOHOL BASE (AND OTHER BERRIES)

This hedgerow vinegar is a fantastic way to use up last year's frozen blackberries before the new lot arrives! Or of course forage for fresh ones. Ensure you include a sizeable portion of sweet berries. This recipe is translatable to any berries, frozen or fresh – the method is the same. Berries are usually rich in yeast and will ferment very quickly without any help, but adding some commercial yeast will ensure complete fermentation.

If your hedgerow blackberries are bland, combine with purchased frozen ones that can be more flavoursome, or something else – raspberries or apples are good choices. You will need to add some sugar – one of the reasons berries are so good for us is their

Blackberries can also be foraged to create vinegar, but this is true of berries generally.

relatively low sugar content! Blackberries do contain tannin and fruit acids, which add some complexity.

Freezing berries first will help the extraction of juice as the thawing process bursts the cells, as will mixing them with some of the sugar before adding water (as a result of osmosis). You could juice them, but unless you have a very efficient centrifugal juicer you might be wasting your time, and you could end up with more pulp than juice. Berries also make excellent infused vinegars (see page 145). You could cook them first as this does soften them considerably, but then you will need to add champagne yeast for fermentation and will lose some bio-actives in the process. As with almost every other recipe, I choose raw.

Ingredients:

Volume	1ltr	2ltr	5ltr
Berries	500g	1,000g	2.5kg
Water	500ml	1,000ml	2.5ltr
Added sugar to 1.060 SG	150g	300g	750g

Method:

- For a raw vinegar, freeze, then defrost the blackberries first, then steep overnight with the added sugar. Then add the water to make up to the required volume – you might not need all of it.
- If cooking, place berries in a saucepan, add sugar and half the water, simmer for five minutes, cool. Add the remaining water to the vessel as needed.
- Proceed to general alcohol fermentation instructions, page 112.

WILD DAMSON ALCOHOL BASE (AND OTHER DRUPES)

This recipe can be adapted to other stone fruits – my favourites are bullaces, which are like giant sloes, or damsons, plums, greengages and Mirabelle plums, alone or in combination. Damsons and bullaces are acidic and tannic and because of this are rarely eaten raw. However, they do make very flavoursome wine. There is nothing more insipid than a supermarket plum, so try to find

Bullaces to make vinegar – the stones can be fished out with a gloved hand.

some real ones, and wait until they are ripe but not rotting – freeze them if you need to collect them as they ripen over several weeks, to stop them going over – this will also help the fruit release their juice upon thawing. They are not suitable for machine juicing or blending.

Cherries can be used in the same way: you could pit them and use them raw (don't eat the pits or blend them so they break because they contain the cyanide precursor amygdalin), or cook them to release the juice. However, unless you have easy access to an abundance, I would opt for using a smaller quantity to flavour a vodka base, or to make an infusion, as then the flavour really stands out.

You can use apricots, peaches and nectarines, but I was not particularly bowled over with these myself – the flavour is too weak to carry above the acetic acid. I would rather put peaches in a salad and dress them with another, more flavoursome vinegar.

Ferment raw fruits if you can easily extract the stones, then you can make the most of the wild yeasts and preserve the bioactive components. If, as is usually the case with wild bullaces, there is almost nothing left after pitting, you can heat them gently in a large pan with a splash of water. As they cook, the flesh will fall away from the stones. They can be strained out using a colander with wide holes – although as the pulp is quite thick, I prefer to put on a rubber glove and fish them out myself.

If you have cooked the fruit, don't forget to add commercial yeast. Tannic damson wine can benefit from a higher alcohol content (you can dilute it later, at the vinegar stage), and also from ageing for up to two years to moderate the astringency – but it is definitely worth the wait! Plums don't require ageing and you can add less sugar for an alcohol base (for SG 1.06).

Ingredients:

Volume	1ltr	2ltr	5ltr
Damsons etc	400g	800g	2kg
Water	400g	800g	2kg
Approx. sugar 1.090 SG or 22° Brix	200g	400g	1kg
Approx. sugar 1.060 SG or 15° Brix	150g	300g	750g

Method:
- Wash and check the damsons (or other drupe).
- Place them in a large pot with the water and heat gently while stirring, until the flesh has softened and the stones are released.
- Leave until cool enough to handle.
- Put on a rubber glove and fish out the stones, or pass the fruits through a colander with large holes, using a potato masher to help separate out the stones.
- Place the pulp directly in a primary fermentation vessel, or into a straining bag first for larger volumes.
- Proceed to general alcohol fermentation instructions, page 112.

KOMBUCHA / TEA ALCOHOL BASE

If you are a kombucha maker, you will be familiar with kombucha vinegar, as it is what you will get if the fermentation goes 'too far'. Despite the similar appearance of the SCOBY and vinegar mother (*see* page 28), kombucha rarely reaches an acidity above 2.5 per cent. There are reasons for this: first, kombucha is usually cultured as a low alcohol beverage so only modest sugar is added – about 50g/ltr, compared with up to 250g/ltr for many wines, limiting

Just a few spoonfuls of tea or some teabags will make a delicious cidery vinegar. How tea vinegar matures to taste like cider is one of the great mysteries of the world.

alcohol and subsequent vinegar production. Then the microbes present in the SCOBY have evolved to function in this low sugar/low alcohol environment, and are usually not tolerant of higher levels.

I would suggest letting your 'old' kombucha vinegar be exactly as it is – a weaker vinegar for quick pickles, diluting it with sparkling water, or as the basis of a delicious drinking vinegar (*see* page 158), and if you want to experiment with tea vinegars at stronger acidity, follow the instructions below for a tea wine. Tea vinegars really do taste delightfully kombucha-like, and at the correct acidity can be used to add an interesting angle to all sorts of pickles.

This will work with any *Camelia sinensis* variety (black, green, white, oolong or pu erh), Earl Grey, Darjeeling, also hibiscus, nettles and so on. The tannins in the tea are useful nutrients for the microbes: tannins are often added as an extra to fruit wines to add 'mouth feel'. You will absolutely need to add brewers' yeast, as there is no source of it in steeped tea! When making kombucha, acidity is added with 'old kombucha'. For this recipe you can add 10 per cent kombucha if you have some, or use lemon juice.

Ingredients:

Volume	1ltr	2ltr	5ltr
Teabags, approx. *or*	3	6	15
Loose-leaf tea	10g	20g	50g
Water	1ltr	2ltr	5ltr
Added sugar measure to SG 1.060 or 15° Brix	150g	300g	750g
Lemon juice or kombucha	50ml 100ml	100ml 200ml	250ml 500ml

Method:
- Place tea or teabags in a large jug with the sugar.
- Boil the kettle and add one-third of the required volume as boiling water.
- Stir well to dissolve the sugar.
- Leave for the recommended steeping time for your tea.
- Add more of the cold remaining water, leaving room for some kombucha or lemon juice to acidify.

- Don't pour boiling hot liquids into glass jars as they can shatter.
- Strain into primary fermentation vessel.
- Proceed to general alcohol fermentation instructions, page 112.

ELDERFLOWER ALCOHOL BASE

Delicate citrussy and delicious, this vinegar is the perfect way to preserve the scent of the short-lived blossoms. You could also do a simple infusion with a wine or spirit vinegar, but this is better. Making elderflower cordial and champagne is an annual ritual for many of us, so it is easy to sideline some for vinegar-making purposes. If you use your own recipe, make sure you know the alcohol content (those ever-important hydrometer readings), or it will be hard to judge how much to dilute it for vinegarising.

As we are submerging the blooms in hot sugar syrup the addition of champagne yeast is required. You can use cold water and rely upon natural yeasts if you prefer; I always did until last year, when my fermentation didn't start.

For more fragrance pick the blooms on a dry sunny day, not after a heavy shower. If you have insect-ridden blooms, put them in a large colander: this can help get rid of the insects quickly. Cover the top with a plate to stop the flowers bouncing out, and bang the colander down on a tray. Many of the bugs should fall out. Repeat this a couple of times.

It is worth sacrificing half a bottle of your elderflower champagne to make this deliciously fragrant vinegar.

To make sure the delicate fragrance is carried through to the final vinegar stage I use significantly more blooms than many recipes specify. This will make an approximately 12 per cent wine that will need to be diluted, but it is too delicious not to make some at the same time!

Elderflower Wine
Ingredients:

30 pristine elderflower heads
700g sugar
120ml lemon juice or three teaspoons of citric acid
4.5ltr water

Method:
- Cut the flowers from the stems.
- Heat the water and sugar in a large saucepan until the sugar is dissolved and the solution just at boiling point.
- Add the flowers and stir them in.
- Leave to cool till manageable.
- Take a hydrometer/refractometer reading and record.
- Leave to infuse during primary fermentation, then strain the flowers.
- Proceed to general alcohol fermentation instructions, page 112.

TOMATO ALCOHOL BASE

If you have ever sliced home-grown summer tomatoes, doused them in olive oil, sprinkled them with salt, and mopped up the juice with some crusty bread, you'll know how utterly delicious real tomato juice is – a world away from tinned or bottled, that's for sure. We are not generally blessed with good availability of decent tomatoes here in the UK. It's a shame, because we can certainly grow them. Track down some local tomatoes or use your own, and preserve that flavour until the next season with this recipe. Tomato vinegar is not only delicious but has high levels of antioxidant activity and vitamin C.[26] The microbiota of tomatoes is not rich in yeasts,[27] so adding some, and some additional nutrition, is a requirement.

If you've ever strained tomato water and discovered how delicious it is, then this vinegar won't disappoint. It is rich in polyphenols too, with high antioxidant activity.

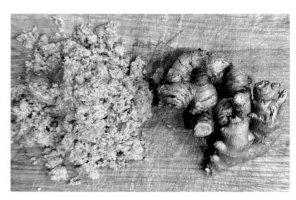

Ginger is something of an acquired taste. It tastes very different to an infused version – hot and peppery. It benefits from a spoonful of sugar if it has been fermented to dryness.

Ingredients:

Volume	1ltr	2ltr	5ltr
Ripe tomatoes	1kg	2kg	5kg
Approx. sugar 1.060 SG, or 15° Brix	150g	300g	750g

Method:
- Wash and drain ripe tomatoes.
- Juice them, or you can ferment a pulp, in which case blitz them in a blender, or manually chop and squash them and put them in a straining bag.
- Proceed to general alcohol fermentation instructions, page 112.

GINGER ALCOHOL BASE

You may be familiar with a 'ginger bug', which is similar in principle to a sourdough starter: fresh ginger is macerated in water mixed with a little sugar that is fed daily; this can be used as a base for all manner of fizzy drinks. I found an abandoned jar of this, and it gave off an amazing vinegary odour: upon tasting it was delicious, so I have deliberately scaled it up. The resulting vinegar is more complex than an infused version, and an interesting addition to a store cupboard. Ginger contains many active yeasts, however I have struggled with stuck alcoholic fermentation, and would suggest the addition of champagne yeast. As

it is not an acidic crop, add some lemon juice to lower the pH to the optimal range. Raisins can add additional nutrients.

Ingredients:

Volume	1ltr	2ltr	5ltr
Ginger	250g	500g	1.25kg
Approx. sugar 1.060 SG or 15° Brix	150g	300g	750g
Lemon juice	50ml	100ml	250ml
Raisins	1tsp	2tsp	5tsp
Water	500ml	1ltr	2.5ltr

Method:
- Macerate the ginger in a food processor, or grate by hand.
- Add water, raisins and lemon juice, stirring well.
- Proceed to general alcohol fermentation instructions, page 112.

GENERIC READY-MADE JUICE ALCOHOL BASE

Almost any preservative-free, ready-prepared fruit or vegetable juice, or even tree sap, can be fermented into first alcohol and then vinegar – including coconut

Use any juice that hasn't been ultra-processed – most have been pasteurised so you will need to add yeast.

Saccharified Vinegars

As previously mentioned, saccharification is a way of releasing sugars contained within starchy vegetables, which can then be used by yeasts to make alcohol. One of the easiest and most effective methods is using koji: this is defined by Robin Sherriff of The Koji Kitchen as follows:

> Koji is a Japanese ingredient that serves as the basis for a huge number of foods and condiments, from soy sauce to saké. It is rice fermented with a specific type of microbe (*Aspergillus oryzae*) to produce enzymes, which open up all sorts of incredible flavours.

Starchy grains including rice and rolled oats can have their sugars released by the action of koji enzymes. You can make your own koji using rice or barley, but that's another story – for now I would purchase online (*see page 172*).

Koji is the Japanese equivalent to malting: a clever way to unlock stored sugar.

water, birch sap, kiwi fruit, mango, pineapple juice – the list is endless. In terms of a recipe, there really isn't one, just a few considerations; then turn to the universal instructions on page 112.

Sugar content: Using the specific gravity tables (*see* page 99) as a reference, 7 per cent alcohol corresponds to approximately SG 1.060/15° Brix, and requires approximately 150g/ltr of sugar. Some juices are sweeter than others: amend accordingly.

Acidity and pH: A pH meter will help you work out whether any additional acidity is required, in which case add lemon juice at the rate of approximately one lemon per litre (about 50ml). Try to maintain a pH range of 3.5 to 4.5.

Nutrients: Complex juice mixtures will be more nutritious – if in doubt add raisins or yeast nutrient.

Yeast: Always add champagne yeast, 1g/ltr to juices, especially packaged ones, as they may have been pasteurised.

KOJI FERMENTATION

Koji fermentation is akin to malting in many ways, as it is a way of creating a natural source of enzymes that can be used in food production to release not just simple sugars from complex starches, but peptides, fatty acids and complex flavours too. It is useful where sugars are 'locked up' in forms that are unavailable to yeasts, for example in starch, which these microbes cannot metabolise. Mixing starchy foods with koji rice allows the enzymes to break down the starch into smaller sugar molecules that can then be utilised by the yeasts.

To make koji, rice (or soya beans, barley or other substrates) is cooked, cooled and inoculated with a specific mould culture, often *Aspergillus oryzae*. You might come across the phrase 'solid-state fermentation' to describe this process.

Koji is thought to have originated in China about three thousand years ago, but has found its home in Japan, where in 2006 it was designated a 'national fungus' due to its importance in so many Japanese foods. Usually we see moulds as a negative presence in our food, something to be avoided at all costs – but just like the strains that exist in blue cheese, koji moulds are incredibly useful to us. *Aspergillus oryzae* is capable of producing around 30 different enzymes, including starch-degrading amylases, protein-cleaving proteases, and even lipases that act upon fats.

Upon inoculation, the presence of starch and nutrients in the rice stimulates mould growth. As the moulds grow at their optimum temperature (between 28 and 36°C is ideal) and optimum humidity (about 90 per cent to start with), a mycelium forms, covering and penetrating the rice. This usually takes around 36 hours. As it grows, the mould produces large quantities of extracellular enzymes; the key is to halt their growth when their enzyme production is at its peak, and before the mould forms spores, which can spoil the flavour of the koji and products that will subsequently be made from it.

This results in the formation of grains of rice that are charged with enzymes – a completely natural product that has many uses when mixed with other food sources; mixing koji rice with cooked rice and water, as we shall see here, will result in amazake with a sugar content upwards of 20 per cent, as the amylase enzymes in the koji cleave the starch molecules in the cooked rice, making simple sugars.

It is possible to influence the growing conditions of koji so that it produces larger quantities of specific enzymes, but for the purposes of releasing sugars for yeast fermentation and alcohol production, the amylases are of greatest interest to us.

RICE/OAT AMAZAKE BASE

Rice vinegar has its origins in Japan. In this recipe we shall be using koji to make amazake as a first stage. This is an incredibly sweet rice drink arising from saccharification; it is purported to have a range of health benefits, despite its enormous sugar content.[28] Do try some before you make the vinegar – you will be quite amazed at the level of sweetness without having added any sugar.

Note: You can also make rice vinegar by converting ready-made rice wine, according to the instructions on page 46.

The challenge when it comes to amazake is maintaining 60°C for eight hours. This is the optimal temperature for action of the amylase enzymes; too low and they won't work efficiently; too high and they will be denatured, which is the equivalent of being 'broken' for an enzyme. If you are lucky, your oven might go low enough, though I strongly recommend using an oven thermometer to check. I use a dehydrating oven that can be maintained at 60°C. An Instant Pot or rice cooker can be used on 'keep warm' mode without the lid on – although again, I would use a thermometer to check. Another option is to pre-warm a thermos flask, heat the amazake to 60°C by stirring constantly in a pan, then add to the flask for the duration.

When you have made the amazake you have the equivalent of a 'must' that can be used for alcoholic

With amazake vinegar, eight hours at 50–60°C is sufficient to break down the starch to sugars.

Amazake vinegar always settles into two layers, but I never strain it – I'd lose half of it!

fermentation. Take a specific gravity or Brix reading: saccharification could produce a sugar content of up to 200g/ltr – that's 1.090 specific gravity or 20° Brix. It is likely that you will need to dilute this down to give 7 per cent alcohol for making vinegar (see page 54).

You will need to add commercial yeast here, as there is no source of it in amazake.

Amazake vinegar separates into two distinct layers – I always leave it like this because it is part of its character, but you could filter it if you wanted to remove some of the nutrients!

Ingredients:

Volume	1ltr	2ltr	5ltr
Rice koji	1 cup	2 cups	5 cups
Steamed white rice (or porridge oats cooked with water)	1 cup	2 cups	5 cups
Water	500ml	1ltr	2.5ltr

Method:

- Place all the ingredients together in a jug or bowl.
- Blitz with a blender (to increase the surface area – this is not strictly necessary).
- Place in a jar in the oven or an instant pot water bath, or directly in a thermos at 60°C.
- Incubate for ten to fourteen hours.
- Measure the sugar content with a hydrometer and dilute if necessary to 1.06 SG by adding a little water at a time and stirring well.
- To finish off, turn to the universal vinegar-making instructions on page 46.

SWEET POTATO VINEGAR

Sweet potatoes may not immediately spring to mind as a starting point for vinegar, but they have a unique property that makes this possible: their high content of the starch-degrading enzyme amylase. If cooked at 75°C they become extremely sweet, as the amylase breaks down starch to maltose, a simpler sugar.[29] In turn, yeast produces another enzyme, invertase, which can break down maltose into its two constituent glucose molecules so alcohol can be created. You could also mix koji with cooked sweet potato to release the glucose, as per the previous recipe, which would maximise the yield, but I find this self-saccharification extremely satisfying (and without the added cost of koji).

Sweet potato flesh is full of sugar when cooked long and slow, made by its own saccharification process.

Method:

- Set the oven to preheat to 75–80°C and check with an oven thermometer that the temperature is correct.
- Wash the sweet potatoes.
- Roast for 60 to 90 minutes.
- Leave to cool.
- Scoop out of the skins.
- Blend with water to make a smooth slurry, and add lemon juice.
- Proceed to general alcohol fermentation instructions, page 112.

WATER KEFIR AND KOMBUCHA VINEGARS

If you grow your water kefir extremely slowly in the fridge, after several months it may well have turned to a beautifully clear, pure-tasting vinegar. You can also make it more quickly by using a cloth cover instead of a sealed jar for your kefir grains, but I find this generates some rather strange flavours. This makes a low-acidity vinegar, usually 1.5 per cent and rarely exceeding 2 per cent, limited by the tolerance of the microbes.

Some raisins will help the microbes get the nutrients they need.

However, kombucha if left will eventually turn to vinegar, for the reason that it will plateau, usually a little higher, at 2.5 per cent. When kombucha becomes too acidic to drink, don't throw it away – you can dilute it to make delicious drinking vinegars, usually about one part kombucha to four parts sparkling water. The added advantage of this is that any residual sugar (and kombucha often retains 3 per cent sugar) will also be diluted 1:4. You will therefore have a drink that is low in sugar yet high in organic acids, including gluconic, glucuronic and acetic. Simply infuse in a jar with a handful of strawberries, raspberries, hibiscus flowers or ginger, then strain, and you will have a drinking vinegar cordial. Store in the fridge to prevent kombucha SCOBY development.

At the fermentation stage you will need to add yeast and some lemon juice or vinegar to lower the pH to the optimal fermentation range of 3.5–4.5. This is not a particularly high-yielding vinegar – rather like the persimmons, it is extremely pulpy and needs to be diluted with two parts water to generate any vinegar at all! Filter a little to check the sugar level – hopefully there will be enough without needing to add any.

Ingredients:

Volume	1ltr	2ltr	5ltr
Large sweet potatoes	3 750g	6 1.5kg	15 3.75kg
Approx. water	400ml	800ml	2ltr
Approx. lemon juice or vinegar	30ml	60ml	150ml

CHAPTER 13

ALL-IN-ONE

With minimal kit requirements, the all-in-one method is suitable for pulps of fruits with high sugar content, lots of yeasts, and soft flesh – persimmon and banana, mango, berries, ripe orchard fruits, dried fruit, also fresh juices and scraps.

Alcohol is still essential for the process, but is produced by yeasts and turned into vinegar by AAB simultaneously. In wild mixtures there will be competition for available sugar: while some will end up as alcohol, some will build yeast populations, be used for cellulose mother, or will feed other microbes.

In turn, vinegar yields are often lower; at completion expect anywhere between 1.5 to 5 per cent acetic acid. Some control over the process is possible – for example, checking sugar content and pH before fermentation begins. You might choose to leave things entirely to nature, or to accelerate the process – the addition of a little vinegar starter would not go amiss; but don't

THE ALL-IN-ONE METHOD

PREPARE A MUST FROM FRUIT JUICE OR PULP
↓
PLACE IN VESSEL LEAVING ROOM FOR EXPANSION
↓
ADD BREATHABLE COVER
↓
STIR DAILY FOR 10 DAYS OR UNTIL VINEGAR SMELLS EMERGE
↓
STRAIN OUT PULP
↓
CONTINUE FERMENTATION FOR APPROX 6 WEEKS
↓
STRAIN
↓
BOTTLE
↓
PASTEURISE (OPTIONAL), AGE OR STORE

Diagram outlining the all-in-one process.

overdo it, as inhibition of yeasts could occur – stick to 20 per cent of the volume and you should be fine.

Room temperature is best for all-in-ones, because lower temperatures are required for yeast activity. Many of these recipes require intervention for the first ten days, in the form of daily stirring to prevent mould development on plant fibres.

You shouldn't need to add any more yeast, but there is no harm in adding a pinch if you feel that nothing is happening (no frothing or yeasty odours after 72 hours).

Remember that all-in-one vinegars are harder to control in terms of final acidity, so may not be suitable for long-term preserving unless you check, and pulpy mixtures will need daily stirring.

All you will need is a cleaned bucket or jar with a breathable cover. Note: although flat vessels are recommended for vinegar production, for all-in-ones a deeper vessel will provide a better environment for yeast growth.

If you are using juice as opposed to pulp, you can also set up an all-in-one continuous culture straightaway – please *see* page 83 for the instructions.

When you have finished with the pulp, freeze it and use it for chutney making when you have a suitably sized hoard. Scraps will not be any good by this time and should be discarded.

ALL-IN-ONE APPLE CIDER VINEGAR

Ingredients

Volume of apple juice	1ltr	2ltr	5ltr
Approximate weight of apples required	2kg	4kg	10kg
Active vinegar mother starter	50ml	100ml	250ml
Approx sugar to 1.060 SG	120g	240g	600g

Or:

Volume of apple pulp	1ltr	2ltr	5ltr
Approximate weight of apples required	1kg	2kg	5kg
Additional water or fruit juice	200ml	400ml	1000ml
Active vinegar mother starter	50ml	100ml	250ml
Approx. sugar to 1.060 SG or 15° Brix	80g	160g	400g

Method:

Prepare juice or pulp as previously for apples and follow the general instructions above, page 125.

SALSAMENTA: FRESH FIG VINEGAR

Let us head back to ancient Rome and Columella's book *De Re Rustica* (*On Rural Affairs*) for this fig vinegar recipe. The Romans were keen on mixing sweet and sour flavours, a concept perfectly captured here. Figs were ubiquitous and featured heavily in the Roman diet. The original recipe is available in Latin for anyone wishing to brush up on their classics translation skills

Figs drying in racks in the sun, in the traditional way. Both dried and fresh figs can be used for vinegar. Fresh fig vinegar is mild and fruity, but the fig flavour comes through more intensely in the dried version.

(on tavolamediterranea.com),[30] and in English below (translated by Harrison Boyd Ash).

There are some regions in which wine, and therefore vinegar also, is lacking. So in the same season of the year green figs in as ripe a state as possible must be picked, especially if the rains have already come on and the figs have fallen to the ground owing to the showers. When they have been gathered, they are stored in jars or pitchers and allowed to ferment there. When they have become sour and have yielded up their moisture, whatever vinegar there is, is carefully strained and poured into sweet-smelling vessels treated with pitch. This liquid takes the place of very sharp vinegar of the first quality and is never affected by decay or mustiness as long as it is not kept in a damp place. Some people prefer quantity to quality, and they will mix water with figs, and from time to time add very ripe fresh figs and allow them to dissolve in the liquid until the flavour of sufficiently sharp vinegar results; after this they let it percolate through small rush baskets or sacking made from broom, and boil the clarified vinegar until they get rid of the scum and every kind of impurity. They then add a little grilled salt, which prevents the production of worms or other animals in it.

So that it's worth the effort, as they are quite dry, here is a quantity, not quality recipe, with a couple of other alterations: we won't store it in vessels lined with pitch, and will probably use a sieve and filter paper rather than sacking! Figs have a rich microbiota including many species of yeast, so I would recommend wild fermentation. As they have a low acid content (usually about pH 5.5), I would recommend an all-in-one method including starter vinegar from the beginning. This will lower the pH to add a little protection from mould, to support optimal yeast growth, and also to add a little moisture, which won't hurt. Use the ripest figs you can get your hands on: ask your greengrocer for a box that are on the cusp of over-ripeness, but before they rot. It will be hard to assess the sugar content so there is no guarantee it will end up at 5 per cent acidity. Add some additional sugar to help.

For dried fig vinegar, turn to the raisin vinegar recipe (*see* page 129).

Ingredients:

Volume	1ltr	2ltr	5ltr
Fresh figs	750g	1.5kg	3.75kg
Sugar	80g	160g	400g
Active vinegar mother starter (optional, approx.)	50ml	100ml	250ml
Water or fruit juice	150ml	400ml	750ml

Method:

- Wash and inspect the figs.
- Cut off the stalks and any mouldy parts.
- Blitz lightly in a blender with sugar, water or juice and vinegar mother (add this little by little to arrive at pH 3.5–4.5).
- Place in an appropriately sized fermentation vessel allowing at least 20 per cent room for expansion. Alternatively, use the figs whole and squish them into the vessel using a spoon or flat-bottomed potato masher to help pack them in/break them up, adding the liquid and sugar as you go.
- Follow the general instructions for all-in-one vinegars (*see* page 125).

PERSIMMON VINEGAR

Persimmon vinegar has strong oriental roots: the fruits may have originated in central and northern China, where more than 800 cultivars exist. It has myriad uses including oil, wine, leaf tea and, of course, vinegar. Not far away, in south-western South Korea, Gam Sikcho (감식초 in Korean) is a vinegar made from Meoski persimmons, which are small, sweet, tannic fruits that thrive there. Traditionally the fruit would be picked before it ripened, steeped in rice wine until softened, strained, and then turned to vinegar with vinegar mother.

Persimmons can even be grown in the UK, though as the trees are sold as 'date plums' you would be forgiven for not realising this. In our shops they are still often labelled 'Sharon fruit', which is the name of one Israeli variety that stuck.

These fruits are ripe enough – they are begging to be fermented.

There are two main types of persimmon: astringent Hachiya, and non-astringent Fuyu. Whilst the latter can be eaten even when barely ripe and firm, astringent varieties are mouth-puckeringly unpleasant until fully ripe; it's easy to spot the end point because they have almost begun to liquefy and are bursting out of their skins.

If necessary you can hasten their ripening by placing them in a paper bag with a couple of bananas, which emit fruit-ripening ethylene. Astringent varieties make the best vinegar, using the simplest imaginable method. All you need are persimmons and nature, and a daily stir. Persimmons usually have a pH of about 4.5, but do check and add either some lemon juice or vinegar to lower the pH if necessary. This is not a particularly high-yielding recipe, so if you can, find a proper greengrocer who might have some going over that you can buy at the close of business – you'll get more for your money.

You must attend to this vinegar daily by stirring until it begins to ferment as it is extremely susceptible to mould. This will be even more likely if temperatures are high, when twice-daily stirring would be advisable. Depending on the juiciness of your persimmons, this can sometimes be too dry – if no liquid is developing,

when the ferment starts to smell of vinegar, the judicious addition of a little water could be required.

Note: During the first few days, this ferment can smell really unpleasant, almost meaty; it's a transition phase and quite normal.

Ingredients:
All you need are very ripe persimmons – preferably Hachiya ones for guaranteed success, however, you can include up to 50 per cent slightly under-ripe or Fuyu fruits, with no deleterious effect. I used twelve very ripe large fruits in a 2ltr jar – you will need extra space as it is an effusive ferment.

Method:
- Remove the calyxes from the persimmons and wash carefully, especially where the calyx was excised.
- Cut them in half and squash them into the jar until half full. The fruits will break up surprisingly easily.
- Check the pH and add a little lemon juice or active vinegar mother to amend to 3.5–4.5 if necessary.
- Follow the general instructions for all-in-one vinegars (*see* page 125).

RAISIN VINEGAR (AND OTHER DRIED FRUITS)

If you consider that raisins are dried grapes, it is fascinating how different raisin and wine vinegar are. This is essentially a store-cupboard vinegar, so can be thrown together without so much as a trip to the shops. I prefer to blitz the raisins to release the sugar and nutrients into the mixture and to stop them floating on the top.

Despite what the science might suggest, I have successfully used raisins with added sulphur dioxide,

You can choose to ferment whole raisins, but I prefer this spectacularly unattractive blitzed alternative – raisins are full of sugar, but the skins do prevent it from becoming freely available for the yeast. The slurry on the left was 13° Brix – enough to make at least a 4 per cent vinegar without any extra sugar.

though of course it is better to use additive-free organic ones. Raisins are one of the sweetest dried fruits, with almost 60 per cent sugar content, so there should be plenty of alcohol to convert to vinegar, and their rich microbiota includes yeasts and AAB. That said, I would still include some active mother-of-vinegar starter, to lower the pH a little and help that fermentation along.

This vinegar is popular in Middle Eastern cookery – you can apply the same principles to dried figs, dates, sultanas and even apricots (the latter are lower in sugar, and adding an additional tablespoon per litre wouldn't hurt). To make a more intensely flavoured vinegar, you could substitute the water with fruit juice – apple would go well here.

Ingredients:

Volume	1ltr	2ltr	5ltr
Dried fruit	300g	600g	1.5kg
Water or fruit juice	600ml	1.2kg	3ltr
Vinegar starter (optional, approx.)	50ml	100ml	250ml

Method:

- Place the ingredients in a blender (for large batches, use a hand blender in situ or work in batches).
- Follow the general instructions for all-in-one vinegars (*see* page 125).

CHAPTER 14

SCRAP VINEGARS

SCRAP ALL-IN-ONE VINEGARS

Apple, quince, pear, pineapple, citrus, beets: all the peels and cores from all of these can be re-purposed to make delicious scrap vinegars, giving a surprising amount of flavour. Although they don't have the intensity of a pure juice version, scrap vinegars are perfect for quick fridge pickles or dressings. Freeze leftovers, either mixed or separately, until you have a good hoard. You can even use the remaining pomace from juicing for this purpose. You could do this as a two-stage process, shutting the lid and making alcohol first, but in terms of the final product I haven't seen any difference. In fact sometimes LAB can take hold in the absence of oxygen and make a slimy gloop.

You will need to add sugar, as peels and cores alone won't have much. I have given an approximate amount to add, which isn't enough to generate 7 per cent, but

Freeze them all! Apples, pears, oranges, lemons, beets, pineapples, bananas.

will most likely yield around 4 per cent alcohol. There is a reason for this: the flavours generated by the apple scraps can be totally overwhelmed in a strong alcohol and resulting strong vinegar. I would suggest that you simply appreciate fruit scrap vinegar for what it is: weaker in flavour yet still delicious.

Scrap all-in-one vinegars require daily stirring for the first couple of weeks, so don't start one if you're going away. I have not included hydrometer testing for these vinegars, as it's slightly tricky – sugar left in the fruit scraps can't really be accounted for, however, there's nothing to stop you checking by blending some pulp and juice.

Ingredients:

Volume	1ltr	2ltr	5ltr
Scraps	1kg	2kg	5kg
Water	To cover		
Lemon juice / raw vinegar	As needed for pH range 3.5–4.5 (optional, but use for beets)		
Added sugar	50g	100g	500g

Method:
- Add water, scraps and sugar to the fermentation vessel, stirring well, or jiggling a spoon around as best you can, to dissolve.
- Follow the general instructions for all-in-one vinegars (*see* page 125).

PINEAPPLE VINEGAR – VINAGRE DE PINA

Pineapple vinegar is popular in South America, and interestingly, is almost always exclusively made from the cores and skins, leaving the pineapple flesh for you to enjoy. That said, if you want to use the flesh you can, it's just not usually done. The alcoholic precursor for this vinegar is also known as tepache, a delicious sparkling drink that can be prepared within a couple of days, often flavoured with cinnamon and chilli. Save up your pineapple peels by freezing them until you

Tepache is a delicious, fermented drink that is the fore-runner for pineapple vinegar. Try not to drink it all!

have a sizeable batch. You should be able to get this fermenting with natural yeasts on pineapple skins. Use at least the skin and core of one fresh ripe pineapple just in case some of the yeasts haven't survived the freezer. Vinegar starter is not usually added, as pineapples are rich sources of AAB, but there is no harm in adding a splash to get things moving.

To tell if a pineapple is ripe, inspect the stem end (the bottom) – make sure it shows no signs of mould, that it yields slightly when pressed, and smells like a ripe pineapple (the same applies to melons, incidentally). A pineapple corer is your friend here, though of course not essential. This is the only recipe in which I have specified which sugar to use; unrefined cane sugar, such as piloncillo or rapadura, is typical, but any dark brown sugar can be substituted. A couple of chillies are a nice addition here.

Ingredients:

Volume	1ltr	2ltr	5ltr
Scraps from	2 pineapples	4 pineapples	10 pineapples
Water	To cover		
Dark brown sugar	120g	240g	600g
Chilli (optional)	1	2	5
Cinnamon stick (optional)	1	2	5
Star anise (optional)	2	4	10

Method:

- Place everything in a suitably sized vessel, with 20 per cent additional capacity in a straining bag for large volumes.
- Follow the general instructions for all-in-one vinegars (*see* page 125).

LET-YOUR-IMAGINATION-RUN-WILD VINEGARS

The vinegars I have described use single ingredients, which I hope has been helpful in terms of the basics, but there's no reason why you can't add whatever you like in whichever combination you please. In this section are some delicious combinations that have been tried and tested by some of the finest fermenters I know! Many are members of the Fermenter's Guild (*see* fermentersguild.org).

Llewyn Máire of Savage Craic made a vinegar using the Japanese-fermented plant extract, kouso, as a base. To this were added wild yeasts from gorse. It's still fermenting, but smells delicious apparently!

Paula Neubauer of Get Pickled Ferments in Frome recycled some sloes that had been steeped in gin, transferring them to cider and then converting that to vinegar. She used 25 per cent previous apple cider vinegar mother as a starter, and fermented it for six weeks at room temperature using the surface method.

Once you have mastered the basics of vinegar and basic wine-making, there is endless potential for experimentation with surplus or foraged wares, or produce that you've grown or purchased specially for the purpose. DR LISA NEWMAN, PAULA NEWBAUER, SIMON

Foraged herbs and flowers make excellent additions to vinegars, either before fermentation, or as infusions. ANNIE SIMPKINS

Vetiver infused with mango vinegar using wood chips. PRATAP CHAHAL

Wild food foraging expert Szymon of Foragerium discovered that ginger with sea buckthorn was an all-in-one delicious combination; he stirred daily until the process was well underway.

Fermentation expert Annie Simkins made a delicious pandan and elderflower vinegar. She told me:

I don't always start out planning to make vinegar, but sometimes I make vinegar accidentally, like this one, which ends up being really special. Every spring I make elderflower champagne from the blossoms in my garden, but last year's batch ended up with a distinctly funky smell, which can often happen when you harvest when it's wet or over-cast. It had a good level of alcohol in it though, so I decided to add some apple cider vinegar 'mother' to it and make vinegar. A few weeks later the funky smell had disappeared and I had some lovely fresh and tart vinegar. I took my experiment even further and infused the vinegar with fresh pandan leaves, which I love to use with its grassy vanilla notes. The two flavours complement each other. This year I'm going to be making elderflower vinegar again, but deliberately not accidentally.

Chef Pratap Chahal at The Hungry Chef has a favourite: a mango vinegar infused with vetiver, an amazing aromatic grass that I had never come across until he kindly sent me some.

Koji-maker Robin Sherriff is pictured here holding up some sake vinegar that he created, simply by the acetic fermentation of sake, a brewed alcohol made from koji. The sake was diluted to 7 per cent, and 20 per cent white wine active vinegar mother starter added.

Sake vinegar in the making. It couldn't be simpler: dilute sake to 7 per cent including 20 per cent active vinegar starter.

CHAPTER 15

VINEGAR FOOD AND FLAVOUR

FLAVOUR, AND HOW WE TASTE VINEGAR

There is one over-riding word that describes the taste of vinegar, and that is 'sour'. A spoonful of vinegar will be lip-puckeringly, wincingly so – to the extent that it might even make your salivary glands hurt!

So why do humans seek out this sensation? 'Sour' is one of five major tastes that we perceive (the others being salty, sweet, bitter and umami), and for at least 10,000 years we have been using fermentation to deliberately make sour flavours. Babies are able to recognise a sour taste, puckering their lips instinctively. A recent study found that all vertebrate species that were tested were able to detect acidity in food, but far fewer liked it, or sought it. The authors hypothesised that the trait may have evolved in fish, who need to sense water acidity for their own survival. The trait was conserved once vertebrates adapted to life on land, although 'why' is harder to answer.

Perhaps the ability persisted to protect creatures from ingesting highly acidic foods; although dangerously acidic foods are not common in nature (they're more likely to be astringent or bitter), some species that are foregut fermenters, such as cows for example, could instinctively need to avoid lowering the

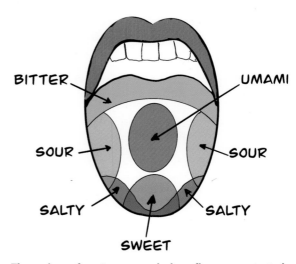

TONGUE TASTE MAP

The regions of our tongue, and where flavours are tasted.

pH of their foregut, to prevent detrimental alterations to their gut microbiota.

Why acidic foods became pleasing for some species (most of whom appear to be hindgut fermenters, as humans, with a colon containing most of the microbiota) could be linked to a way of attracting us to foods that were more likely to be nutritious, containing vitamin C for example. Or they might be linked to man's ability to survive in challenging nutritional environments by eating over-ripe fruit, in a state of yeast, lactic acid and acetobacter-driven decay. This would have been a novel source of safe calories, due to the protective nature of acidic foods, giving humans a selective advantage. In fact, fondness for acidic foods might have led to the eventual control of rotting, and the development of fermentation.[53]

Acid-responsive receptors are found on our taste buds. Eating sour foods has also been linked to the release of the mood-regulating neurotransmitter serotonin: an experiment using green glowing proteins that fit serotonin receptors on nerve cells showed the highest concentration of these on the part of the tongue where sour tastes are detected. The researchers concluded that serotonin relays information to the brain that food is sour.[54]

Even with our predilection for sweet, salty flavours these days, sour is still much in abundance, as a

component of almost every sauce, salad dressing, piece of fruit, spoonful of yoghurt, and in chutneys, pickled onions and gherkins too. With the massive resurgence of interest in fermented foods, kombucha, kimchi, kefir, sauerkraut, sourdough and raw vinegars are on the menu and our 'sour' receptors are getting the use they deserve.

VINEGAR IN COOKING

Vinegar is best known to most of us as a culinary ingredient – we often have a few different bottles of it, usually in response to a particular recipe demanding sherry, balsamic or cider vinegar. They might sit there inertly for years, like biro pen tops underneath a microwave, until the amount of sediment gathering at the bottom prompts their disposal. I carried out a local survey of my customer base to determine how many vinegars people with at least a mild interest in cooking had in their kitchen cupboards – the results are

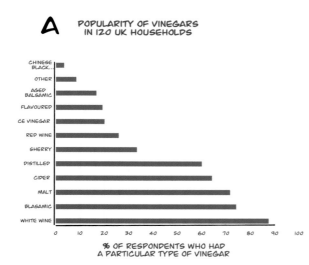

A POPULARITY OF VINEGARS IN 120 UK HOUSEHOLDS

% OF RESPONDENTS WHO HAD A PARTICULAR TYPE OF VINEGAR

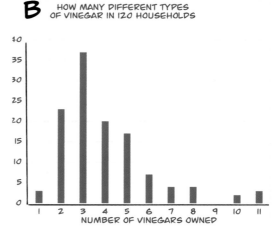

B HOW MANY DIFFERENT TYPES OF VINEGAR IN 120 HOUSEHOLDS

NUMBER OF VINEGARS OWNED

An Instagram survey was carried out to determine which was the most popular vinegar, and how many different types people had.

shown below for a) the number of vinegars and b) the distribution of vinegars owned.

As the figure shows, everyone had at least two types of vinegar: the most common was white wine, then balsamic, followed by apple cider vinegar, and in fourth place our national speciality, malt vinegar. When asked which was the favourite, balsamic was the clear winner, likely due to its deep caramelly undertones and sweetness.

The chef and cookery writer Mark Diacono has described vinegar as 'the magical element that will transform your cooking'. We add vinegar to our food because it stimulates our palates and awakes our taste buds. It brightens and enhances other flavours, yet can balance at the same time: fat (salad dressings), sweet (strawberries and balsamic vinegar) and salt (salt 'n' vinegar crisps) can all be married with it.

Vinegar and Protein

Vinegar can be help you make perfect poached eggs. A splash added to the poaching water stabilises protein cross-links in the albumen (egg white). Increasing the acidity of the water lowers the temperature at which the egg whites will coagulate, so the process happens faster. Chemically speaking, it brings albumin closer to its iso-electric point, where it is least soluble in water. The same stabilising effect occurs when whisking meringues.

In cheese making, vinegar is used to coagulate milk proteins (this also works with lemon juice, which contains citric acid). Milk consists of proteins, sugars and fats. Normally its protein molecules repel each other, existing separately in the whey, and the milk appears homogenous. When vinegar is added, the number of positively charged hydrogen ions in the solution increases. These ions bind to the protein molecules, causing them to attract other protein molecules, forming lumps of curd. This process happens more quickly at warmer temperatures. Queso Blanco, Mozarella and ricotta-style cheeses all involve the addition of vinegar (or lemon juice).

Vinegar as a Tenderiser

Vinegar can tenderise meat and is often used in marinades as it promotes acid hydrolysis of the meat proteins. There are two main proteins in meat fibres:

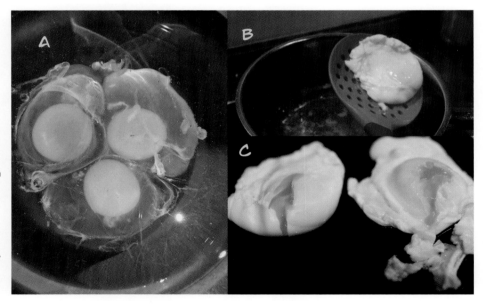

It really does make a difference! An alternative method (a) is to soak the eggs in a solution of 100ml water containing 1 to 2tbsp of vinegar. When the outer layer begins to 'set', they can be removed to the pan for cooking. (b) and (c) show how much better they hold their shape with a little vinegar.

actin and myosin. Myosin breaks down more easily: the proteins are broken into smaller peptides, which can bond with each other and trap liquid into the meat, making it juicy and tender. However, if marinated for too long, the structural actin filaments will denature – if these break down, the sequestered moisture will be lost and the meat will toughen.

It can also be used to 'cook' thinly sliced fish ceviche, although as no heat is involved it isn't exactly the same as conventional cooking. Here, the addition of acid causes the proteins to denature, resulting in raw fish with the opaque appearance and texture of cooked fish.

Vinegar as a Wine Substitute

In recipes where long slow cooking is required, the acidity and complexity provided by a bottle of wine can be replaced with a couple of tablespoons of your finest, most complex vinegar.

WORLD-FAMOUS VINEGARS

As we have seen, vinegar is everywhere, a worldwide phenomenon, but some vinegars are more famous than others! Here are the tales of four of the world's best loved: balsamic, Chinese black, sherry and malt.

Balsamic Vinegar

Almost everyone has a bottle of balsamic vinegar in the cupboard, its rich, complex undertones making it a popular choice for a range of recipes. It is rather an exception when it comes to vinegar, as it is not made directly from either wine or fruit juice, but from boiled grape must, which is then fermented and aged. 'Grape must' comprises the juice, skins and pips of pressed grapes.

PDOs, DOPs and IGPs

DOP (denominazione d'origine protetta) – or in English PDO (protected designation of origin) – means that a food can only be produced in a specific geographical region, according to traditional methods. Examples include Balsamic Vinegar Tradizionale and Vinagre de Jerez, and it also applies to items such as wine, cheese and meat.

Balsamic vinegar originated in the environs of Modena, a town in the Emilia-Romagna region of northern Italy. The origin of the name seems to be derived from 'balsam' or 'balm', which are other names for a soothing salve or ointment – perhaps relating to times when the plague was rampant and its use was widespread as a prophylactic. Its exact origins are vague, however in *De Re Rustica* Roman author Columella mentions a *cella defruitaria* (an acetaria, or cellar where wine is boiled), and also that cooked must, once cooled, is poured into amphorae and left for one year.

The process was developed further in the Middle Ages when wooden barrels became commonplace. In 1598, the duke of the duchy moved to Modena, where home production of this delicious vinegar was in full

Thick, syrupy, aged balsamic. It takes years of evaporation and concentration to reach this point. SHUTTERSTOCK

swing; realising its potential, he set up his own acetaria. It is not clear when exactly the ageing process began, but in 1747 the term 'balsamico' was first mentioned in a register of the ducal cellar. Perhaps down the generations, dukes were able to taste the aged product and realised that this was where the magic lay.

Whilst the term 'balsamic vinegar' can be very loosely used, there are three types with PDO status: Aceto Baslamico Tradizionale di Modena DOP (traditional balsamic vinegar of Modena); Aceto Baslamico Tradizionale Reggio Emilia DOP (traditional balsamic vinegar of the Emilia region); and Aceto Balsamico di Modena IGP (balsamic vinegar of Modena).

Vinegars labelled 'tradizionale' are made using the age-old process; others are blended with white wine vinegar, though still produced in this region – some versions contain as little as 1 per cent grape must. There is a huge range in the cost of balsamic vinegar, from over £1,000 a litre to just a couple of pounds for a 1 per cent solution. The following description of the making process might make it clearer why it can be so costly.

Traditional balsamic vinegar is made according to a series of strict regulations. The must from ripe red and white grapes grown in the region of designation (for example Trebbiano or Lambrusco) is processed as follows:

- The juice is separated from the skins and seeds and filtered.
- The must is brought to a boil and simmered gently over an open flame for 24 hours, until it has reduced to a third of its original volume with a sugar content of approximately 30 per cent.
- Cooled must is inoculated with yeasts and the mother of vinegar to start the fermentation process.
- This starter vinegar is transferred to a horizontally placed wooden barrel known as a batteria, the first in a series of at least five barrels of decreasing size, made from different woods: oak, ash, cherry, chestnut and juniper, each of which will impart a different flavour.

- The barrels are kept in a warm environment to facilitate slow evaporation from the liquid.
- None of the vinegar can be withdrawn before the minimum ageing period, which is twelve years.
- After that time, some vinegar is removed from the smallest barrel and replaced with an equal quantity of vinegar from the previous barrel, and so on, until freshly boiled must is added to the largest barrel. This continuous process is known as 'solera', and is also employed in making brandy and sherry.

The ageing process makes traditional balsamic vinegar unique – the flavour intensifies with time, evaporation, storage in wooden barrels, and the topping-up process, concentrating the flavours and reducing the must to a thick, syrupy consistency. It takes about eighteen gallons of boiled must to produce, twelve years later, just one gallon of 'Balsamico Tradizionale'. Some bottles are aged for 25 years, and these are labelled as 'extravecchio'. Certification is required before these products can be bottled and sold.

The rules for Aceto Baslamico di Modena IGP are much more relaxed; grapes can come from anywhere, and if they're processed in Modena, the bottles can be filled anywhere too. It only needs to be aged for 60 days, and woodchips can be used to help with flavouring.

White Condiment

White condiment used to be called white balsamic vinegar but has recently been renamed white condiment because of legal issues. It is derived from the soft pressing of Trebbiano grapes, with the skins removed, which delivers a particularly sweet juice. Grapes are cooked at high pressure and low temperature, and blended with high quality, white wine vinegar. Ageing in wood barrels of a light colour, or even stainless steel, preserves the pale colour. This fruity, floral and sweet vinegar is a newer addition, dating from the early 1900s.

Chinese Zhenjiang (Black) Vinegar

Originating in the city of Zhenjiang, Jiangsu province, during the Tang dynasty (AD600–900), Zhenjiang is probably China's most internationally famous vinegar, although there are others (Shanxi and Yongchun, for example).

Chinese vinegars use starches, including rice and grains, instead of fruit, and unlike most other vinegars of note, contain a mixture of ingredients – for example in black vinegar, a combination of rice, wheat, barley and pea.

However, the overarching principles are same, in that alcohol is produced and converted into vinegar – though beforehand, an additional saccharification step is needed to release sugars from the starchy grains. Helpful moulds such as *Aspergillus oryzae* produce massive amounts of amylase enzyme, which break down starch into its component glucose molecules, making them readily accessible for yeast alcoholic fermentation. The following stages are involved:

- A dry mash of grains is steamed. Then comes the addition of something specific to Chinese vinegar production: Qu, a solid block of pre-mixed moulds and yeasts for simultaneous saccharification and alcohol production. The reaction releases quantities of heat, which is released by transferring the mash between vessels for about five days.
- Pellets of pei are added: these are small blocks of AAB made from dried vinegar. After two weeks of daily stirring, salt is added to halt any further fermentation, and the mixture is left to sit in the sun for several days.
- Three washing stages separate the vinegar from the solid-state mass. The first wash generates the most concentrated, prized vinegar, while the third wash is used to make more pei for subsequent fermentations.
- The washings are aged in vats for at least six months, and up to six years for the finest vintage. During the ageing process the Maillard reaction, which is the result of the interaction between proteins and carbohydrates, turns the vinegar the densest black.

Here, with the light shining through and compared to malt vinegar, black vinegar is…black! Even this thin, salty vinegar is really dark.

The flavour of black vinegar is quite unique, salty and malty – almost no other vinegars have salt added. It doesn't have PDO status, but most of it does still come from the region.

Vinagre de Jerez (Spain)

With its unmistakeable sherry flavour, there is no hiding the base product here. With its PDO status, it can only be manufactured in the environs of Jerez in Andalusia, where viticulture was introduced about 3,000 years ago by the Phoenicians. It has more residual alcohol than most other vinegars, and with commonly up to 7 per cent acidity, a stronger taste.

Sherry, and thus the resulting vinegar, is made exclusively from three grape varieties: 98.5 per cent Palomino, with just 1 per cent Moscatel and 0.5 per cent Pedro Ximénez. Ideal conditions prevail here for their growth: a microclimate with 300 days of annual sunshine and humidity brought by the easterly winds from the Atlantic Ocean. This region is rich in albariza, a unique Andalusian soil named from the word *albarizo*, meaning 'off-white' in Spanish. It is composed of mostly calcium carbonate, with some clay and sand, and can appear dazzling white in the dry summer months. When it rains, albariza absorbs water like a sponge. In the sunshine, the topsoil bakes into a hard crust, trapping any remaining water below, which slowly releases moisture to the vines as they grow, so there is no need for irrigation.

The white albariza soil of Jerez provides the perfect conditions for sherry grapes. SHUTTERSTOCK

Sherry is a fortified wine, which develops its flavour in a series of barrels via the solera system, often under a waxy cuticle formed by yeasts called 'flor': this is interesting because it is similar to the yeast pellicles that can sometimes be found on the surface of vinegar, although we get rid of them! Neutral grape spirit is added to increase alcohol content. Jerez vinegar follows the same barrel-ageing process as sherry, with similarities to balsamic vinegar. The process takes up to twenty years.

Wooden barrels are stacked on their sides: in the first stage, the oldest vinegars are at the bottom of the pile, on the floor, called the solera, which is where the method gets its name from (suelo means 'floor' in Spanish). Newer barrels lie in rows on top. An amount of vinegar for bottling is removed from the casks on the solera. The amount removed is replaced by younger vinegar from the next row up, the first criadera, and this is then replaced with vinegar from the next row up, the second criadera.

There are several different grades of Vinagre de Jerez, according to the length of cask ageing:

- Sherry vinegar is aged for 6 to 24 months, with a total acidity of 7 per cent and up to 3 per cent alcohol. It is an intense amber colour.
- Sherry vinegar riserva is aged for two to ten years, so its flavours are more pronounced with a longer after-taste.
- Sherry vinegar gran reserva is aged for more than ten years, with at least 8 per cent acetic acid and

a fully rounded taste. It must be assessed by the regulatory council to 'earn' its label.

Malt Vinegar

Malt vinegar is the United Kingdom's primary vinegar and is a defining characteristic of many of our best-known dishes including fish and chips, pickled onions and chutneys. In fact, malting is very similar to the same process of saccharification that is seen in Chinese vinegar production, facilitating the conversion of starches in the grains to sugars for alcoholic fermentation. I carried out a survey to determine what proportion of my Instagram followers had any idea what malt was or how it was made. An astonishingly low proportion of respondents – just 11 per cent of 150 – knew the answer, so if you don't know, you are not alone! See the insert below 'What is Malt' for more information.

In the early days of malt vinegar production, vinegar would have been closely associated with the local brewing industry, spoiled batches of beer being the starting point for production. These days, vinegar manufacturers use malt grown specifically for the purpose; for Sarson's, the UK's largest malt vinegar producer, this is always of British origin.

- To extract the sugars necessary for alcoholic fermentation, malted barley is milled, then transferred to a grist hopper.
- The grains are cracked and mashed in hot water to extract the sugars.
- The resulting mash is cooled and fed through to a fermenter, where yeast is added. (This is simpler than making beer, where the wort is boiled and hops added for additional flavour.)
- During a six-day fermentation process, sugars from the malt are converted to alcohol.
- The liquid is fed to the acetifier. Sarson's uses pine vats full of larchwood wool, which provides an inert support for the AAB. It doesn't discolour the vinegar as other types of wood can.
- After a seven-day aerated and temperature-controlled fermentation, the vinegar is ready.

WHAT IS MALT?

Malt is barley, or other grain, that has been steeped, germinated and dried, and used for brewing or distilling and vinegar making. The Maltsters' Association of Great Britain describes malting as 'the controlled germination of cereals, followed by a termination of this natural process by the application of heat'. Malting is a form of saccharification, and one of the earliest examples of biotechnology, dating back to Egyptian times, about 4000BC.

Barley for malting must be capable of germination, so sourcing a product of excellent quality is essential.

A barley kernel is composed of three parts:

- The embryo, or germ, that will grow into the acrospire; roots and shoots.
- The endosperm that comprises insoluble starch, the food reserve to be used by the germ; starch is about 80 per cent of the weight of the grain.
- The husk that covers the grain surface to protect it.

There are several stages involved in the process:

- Grain is stored for a minimum of six weeks to allow it to overcome dormancy.
- It is then hydrated by steeping in water. The correct combination of water and air are required to result in the ideal moisture content for germination and modification of the starchy endosperm.
- The steeped grain is transferred to a germination vessel, which used to be the germination floor where the grain was turned by shovel to prevent the build-up heat by the action of the enzymes in the grains – these days, this is done by mechanical turner. The process takes about five days – until the enzymatic activity is great enough to have modified the starch, but before the endosperm can be converted into glucose. The process is stopped by the application of heat.
- The modified green malt is then kiln dried, which halts the enzymatic process, and the resulting product is now called malt.
- It's not ready to use yet, though. Malt from the kiln is processed in a deculmer to remove the 'culm' or small rootlets that emerge during germination (this can be used for animal feed).
- The malt is then ready for use by brewers and vinegar makers.

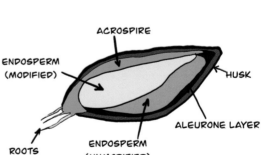

A BARLEY KERNEL DURING GERMINATION

ACROSPIRE

ENDOSPERM (MODIFIED)

HUSK

ALEURONE LAYER

ROOTS

ENDOSPERM (UNMODIFIED)

Sprouted malt grains, and an in-depth view of the barley kernel, showing the growing acrospire that would develop into shoot and root, the nutrient-rich aleurone layer, and the endosperm where the starch is stored, part modified, part unmodified. The kernel is contained within a hard husk. WIKIMEDIA COMMONS

DISTILLED (SPIRIT) VINEGAR

Almost everyone's kitchen has a bottle of white distilled (or spirit) vinegar. It's the type we tend to use for pickling or cleaning, and is usually colourless. But whereas wine and cider vinegars are clear about their origins, 'distilled' doesn't tell us much. The name implies that the vinegar has been distilled in some way, but this is misleading: it means that the vinegar is made from distilled alcohol, or spirits. In fact the ingredients that have been used to make the distilled alcohol aren't important – it could be beer, wine, or alcohol produced from the fermentation of grains, sugar beet, corn, molasses, even whey, whatever is cheap and available – it merely describes a source of alcohol that is purified by the process of distillation (*see* inset 'Fractional Distillation' below).

Distilled vinegar became popular when quick generator methods were established in the 1860s and it was discovered that cheap starting materials could be easily converted into distilled spirits and then to vinegar. Its discovery had the unfortunate consequence of out-competing artisan and traditional-method vinegar producers of those times, putting many out of business.

FRACTIONAL DISTILLATION

Fractional distillation is a process for separating the components of a liquid mixture using differences in boiling points and condensation. Alcohol has a boiling point of 78.37°C, compared with 100°C for water. A piece of apparatus called a still is needed, the earliest examples of which date to Babylonian times.

There are three basic elements: a boiling vessel with heater, a column and a condenser, and three basic steps:

- First, the mixture is heated into a vapour.
- Second, the vapour rises through the fractionated column, falling back as it reaches cold glass – each time it falls back it meets more vapour starting to rise, increasing the concentration of alcohol, so over a few minutes, the concentration continues to increase until it contains enough pure alcohol vapour to reach the top of the column.

- Third, it reaches the cold surface of the condenser, which turns it back into a liquid, which is collected. This is now a solution of ethanol in water, which can reach concentrations of up to 96 per cent.

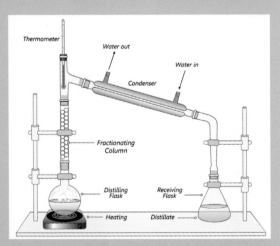

Setting up a still at home would require these components. SHUTTERSTOCK

CHAPTER 16

USING YOUR HOME-MADE VINEGARS

Your home-made vinegars can be used and enhanced in all sorts of ways: cook with them, clean with them, enhance your health with them…

VINEGAR IN THE KITCHEN

The fields of food and medicine merge beautifully here, with preparations that are both delicious and remedial. The boundaries of how to define a cooking, pickling or drinking vinegar, oxymel, shrub or switchel are blurred – I've tried below, but if you want to drink plum vinegar, or cook with rhubarb shrub, then please do not feel constrained by these labels!

Cooking vinegar: Any vinegar of 5 per cent (usually), 7 per cent acidity (rarely, for example, sherry vinegar); usually stalwarts of the kitchen, for example wine vinegars, distilled white vinegar, rice wine vinegar, malt vinegar.

Pickling vinegar: High acidity (6 per cent). Can be purchased especially for the purpose with added spices (but you can use your own at 5 per cent acidity or above). Pickles can be stored for up to a year.

Quick-pickling vinegar: Lower acidity and raw vinegars with less preserving power for immediate use, and short-term storage pickles.

Vinegar infusion: Vinegars infused with herbs, spices and fruits, usually not sweetened.

Now you have made vinegars, use them – on everything!

Crema di aceto: A syrupy, sweet, fruit-based vinegar infusion that is heated during preparation.

Shrub: A concentrated vinegar-based fruit cordial, or drinking syrup for dilution, popular in cocktails since the nineteenth century. The name is derived from the Arabic, *sharāb*, which means syrup. It was originally a way of preserving excess fruit, the addition of large quantities of sugar and vinegar preventing degradation. Shrubs are often, though not exclusively, cold steeped.

Oxymel: The *oxy* part of the word means 'acid' and *mel* means 'honey'. These medicinal tonics were used by the ancient Greeks and may have evolved as a way of extracting and using herbs that tasted unpleasant. Herbs and spices are infused into a mixture of honey and vinegar, which serve as solvents for the extrusion of plant phytochemicals. They are often used in herbal medicine, though are equally useful for drinking or cooking with.

Switchel: A ginger-based vinegary drink, also known as 'Haymakers' punch', dating back to the 1700s.

INFUSED VINEGARS

Use infused vinegars to lock in the flavours of your favourite herbs and flowers to last you through the winter, or make complex mixtures such as fire cider – the opportunities are infinite.

Which Vinegar to Use

Choose a vinegar that will complement, rather than overpower: a plain rice or white-wine vinegar for a simple herb, a hearty red-wine vinegar with juniper and rosemary, or basil leaves in a tomato vinegar.

There are a couple of additional considerations: use a vinegar with at least 5 per cent acidity to prevent the growth of unwanted microbes. And if you use a raw vinegar, an infused vinegar flavour could fade more quickly due to low-level continued microbial activity. For stability, I would recommend pasteurising vinegar before infusing, or refrigerate it afterwards. Below are some ideas for infusions.

Floral vinegars: The petals of chives, nasturtiums, dandelions, hibiscus, roses, elderflowers, or the leaves of scented geraniums or figs.

Herb vinegars: Rosemary, tarragon, thyme, oregano, marjoram, basil and fennel.

Fruits and vegetables: Wild garlic, fresh garlic, black garlic, citrus peels, seaweed.

Almost any combination of herb, fragrant petal, spice, ingredient used for flavouring, can be infused into vinegar.

Roses, scented geraniums, elderflowers, also dried hibiscus flowers will add flavour, and in the case of the latter, a lot of colour.

Making a Simple Infusion

Ensure that your glassware is sterile (*see* page 41). Simply add a handful of chopped herbs or petals to about 250ml of 5 per cent vinegar of your choice. If you heat the vinegar before using it to just below boiling point, the result will be more stable. However, this is not essential. Cool before adding to the herbs. Leave to infuse in a cool place for two weeks, shaking it whenever you pass it. After that time, strain and decant into a fresh sterilised bottle. Store at room temperature for up to a year, or until the flavour fades (these keep longer than pickles because the vegetable matter has been removed).

Four Thieves' Vinegar

In the eighteenth century the plague was rife in Toulouse, France. Apparently, four thieves who robbed the homes and cadavers of plague victims repeatedly avoided infection by the plague-carrying microbe *Yersinia pestis*. Eventually they were caught, and the reason for their apparent immunity was traded for their freedom. They revealed that they had been imbibing a special vinegar blend comprising white wine vinegar, wormwood, meadowsweet, juniper berries, wild marjoram, sage, cloves, elecampane root, angelica, rosemary and horehound, and camphor. Below is a simpler version of this recipe, though hopefully you won't need it for warding off the plague! This concoction is delicious as an aperitif with a mixer. Use either fresh or dried herbs, or a mixture; for fresh herbs, multiply up the quantities by a factor of three.

Ingredients:

500ml of 5 per cent acidity vinegar (preferably your own ACV or white wine vinegar)
2tsp rosemary
1tsp juniper
1tbsp marjoram
1tsp lavender
2 bay leaves
2tsp sage
1tbsp thyme

There is a tendency for the herbs to get stuck in the lid if you shake vigorously, so an occasional stir is preferable. Infuse for at least a fortnight for full flavour development before straining.

2tsp mint
1tsp cloves
1tsp black peppercorns

Method:

- Chop fresh herbs to increase the surface area.
- Place ingredients in a sterilised 1ltr jar with a lid.
- Warm the vinegar to approximately 60°C.
- Add to the jar and seal (if you have a metal lid put some greaseproof paper between the lid and the jar, or it will go rusty as the vinegar reacts with the metal).
- Leave in a cool dark place for 2–4 weeks.
- Strain and store in the same environment.

Plum Vinegar Infusion – Crema di Aceto di Prugna

This is one of the most delicious vinegars I have come across, a marriage of white-wine vinegar, Victoria plums and sugar, which is almost like a syrup. Your salads will never be the same again.

Ingredients:

500g plums
300g white-wine vinegar (or other 5 per cent home-made vinegar)
200g sugar
1 cinnamon stick

Method:

- Add vinegar and sugar to a pan, and stir until dissolved.
- Pit the plums, either before cooking, or strain them out after.
- Add them to the mixture and simmer for 10min.

Deliciously sweet, drink this vinegar diluted with a mixer or dress you salads with it.

- Cool.
- Strain through a bag.
- Keep in a bottle out of direct sunlight.

Variations

This method works with, among others, fresh or frozen figs, cherries or peaches, bullaces, blackberries, strawberries, redcurrants and rhubarb. Add cloves and ginger for extra warmth.

USING YOUR VINEGAR FOR PICKLING

A few pickles as a side dish or starter are an excellent daily 'shot' of vinegar. Onions, gherkins, capers, carrots, cauliflower, aubergine, mushrooms, water-melon rinds, beetroot, even eggs can all be submerged in vinegar for enhanced deliciousness. Do ensure that you have at least one side of a piece of vegetable less than 2cm thick, so that the vinegar can penetrate and preserve.

There are two methods with a subtle yet important difference:

- Quick pickling requires lower concentrations of acetic acid, so you can use home-made vinegar without knowing the acidity. The pickles need to be refrigerated to prevent spoilage, and should be consumed within two weeks.
- Regular pickling is for longer storage – up to a year. Higher acidity vinegar is required – 5 to 8 per cent, the jars must be sterile, and the pickles require heating and then cooling in the jars to seal them. For long-term storage, jars should be treated by water-bath canning. For more information, there are several resources on this on the internet. Without this additional step, keep them in the fridge for up to three months.

Pickling recipes abound on the internet, many of which seem to include water, which dilutes the preserving power of the vinegar. This essentially turns the recipe into a 'quick pickle' recipe, so do be sure to refrigerate them and consume within a couple of weeks.

Just a Note about Pickling

The term 'pickle' can have different connotations. It can be used to describe vegetables that have been preserved in vinegar, but also those that have been lacto-fermented. These two might have the same name, but functionally they are quite different. Lacto-fermentation is a process whereby foods are acidified, nutritionally enhanced, and preserved by the action of LAB, which are also microbes that could be probiotic. In fact I have written another book on this very subject: *Fermented Foods, a Practical Approach*, also published by The Crowood Press. Pickles in vinegar, especially if pasteurised, will not have this nutritional advantage. They will still be delicious, however, and of course contain vinegar that can positively influence blood sugar, but this is less effective if the pickles are sweetened.

Quickest of Quick Pickles

This is a perfect way to showcase home-made vinegars, and with no heating, preparation takes only moments. I never add sugar because I find it unnecessary, but it is an optional extra. Daikon radishes are perfect here – they seem to absorb just the right amount of acidity, but do substitute whatever vegetables are at hand.

The quickest and most delicious of quick pickles – but don't be constrained by my suggestions: almost anything edible can be quick pickled.

Ingredients:

500g daikon or other radish and carrots
Slivers of garlic
A teaspoon of grated ginger
500ml vinegar of your choice (raw beet vinegar works well)
2tsp sugar (optional)

Method:

- Julienne or shred the vegetables, or cut into thin pieces of pie and place in a clean jar.
- Cover with vinegar and leave to infuse for a couple of hours in the fridge. Keeps for up to a week.

Pickled Courgettes

As one of the most over-produced allotment vegetables, I was overjoyed when I discovered that courgettes pickle beautifully. The trick is to peel them in ribbons. If the seeds are enormous, scoop them out as they are rather floppy. Quince, white wine or cucumber vodka vinegar pair well, but I am sure anything will do!

Ingredients:

500g courgettes, peeled into ribbons (put the seeds in with your next bean chilli etc.)
2tsp coriander seeds
500ml pale vinegar at 5 per cent acidity
1tbsp sugar (optional)

Ribbons of courgettes for pickling. I am not sure why this is so much more successful than cutting them in discs, but it seems to be.

2tsp mustard seeds (any type)
1 clove garlic, crushed
1tsp each of black pepper and salt

Method:

- Heat all the ingredients except the courgettes in a pan over a medium heat until just boiling.
- Leave to cool.
- Place the courgette strips in a sterilised jar.
- Pour over the cooled liquid.
- Refrigerate for two weeks for the best flavour, but can be eaten right away. Use within a month.

Note: Don't pour hot liquid on to the courgettes as they will cook and go soggy.

Dill-Pickled Beetroot

You'll never have to buy those sad, plastic vacuum-packed examples again! Baby beets are prettiest, but you can neatly slice, dice or julienne larger ones. You will need a 1ltr jar.

Ingredients:

500g cleaned beets
500g red or white vinegar (the white vinegar will turn red anyway!)
1tbsp crushed juniper berries

1tsp each of black pepper and salt
1 handful of fresh dill
1 red onion
2tbsp sugar (optional)

Method:

- Cook the beets by either boiling, roasting, microwaving or pressure cooking until they can be pierced easily with a knife.
- Peel away the skins and chop as desired.
- Put the beets in the jar with the dill and red onion.
- In a pan heat the vinegar, sugar if using, salt, pepper and juniper berries until just boiling.
- Pour hot liquid over the beets and seal the jar quickly.
- When cool, refrigerate and use within three months.

Quick-Pickled Magnolia Blossoms

Perhaps magnolia flowers are too beautiful to be picked and pickled, but if you have some to spare, they have an interesting gingery flavour. Quick pickling with a weaker scrap vinegar works here, otherwise the delicate flavour can be overpowered. If you don't have any, this is one recipe where I would dilute the vinegar.

Gingery and delicate, remember not to overpower these with a strongly flavoured pickling liquid.

Ingredients:

10 magnolia blooms, with the petals removed from the base

300ml scrap vinegar (or rice, white wine, ACV diluted 50/50 with water)

½tbsp salt

1½tbsp sugar

Method:

- Sterilise a jam jar or Kilner jars with 500ml capacity.
- Place the magnolia petals in the jars.
- Heat the vinegar, sugar and salt to boiling point, stirring well.
- Pour over the magnolia petals.
- Quickly seal the lid – you'll get a better seal as it cools.
- When cooled, keep in the fridge for a fortnight.

Pink Pickled Onions

The colour of these onions alone makes them an irresistible accompaniment to anything!

Ingredients:

3 small red onions, very finely sliced in rings (use a mandolin and glove if you have them)

300ml pale vinegar (rice, white wine, ACV, quince etc.)

A pinch of dried chilli (optional)

1½tbsp sugar

½tbsp salt

1tsp mustard seeds (any type, optional)

Method:

- Place the onion rings in the jars.
- Heat the vinegar, sugar, salt and spices to boiling point, stirring well.
- Pour over the onions.
- Quickly seal the lid – you'll get a better seal as it cools that way.
- When cooled keep in the fridge for up to a month.

Vinegar-Lovers' Salad Dressing

An essential three-ingredient dressing that doesn't need any extra sugar, perfect for those of us who have made vinegars and want them to be tasted! All vinegars will work, but those with a residual sweetness work best. If you are using a scrap vinegar with lower acidity, you might need to add a little more. The mustard is a great emulsifier.

Ingredients:

100ml extra virgin olive oil

75–100ml home-made vinegar, depending on acidity

2 heaped tsp grain or Dijon mustard

Salt and pepper to taste

Essential fridge fare and ready in moments.

Method:

- Mix everything together in a bowl, and decant into a clean bottle.
- Refrigerate and use within two weeks (keep in the fridge door, so that the oil doesn't set).

Fruit-Pulp Chutney Recipe

Fruit pulp that you have strained out of a primary or all-in-one fermentation may still have both structure and flavour left! I've adapted my apple chutney recipe so that you can substitute just about anything else for the apples.

Ingredients:

1kg apples and/or fruit pulp
500g onions
100g sultanas
500ml white wine/malt/ACV
250g sugar
10g sea salt
25g grated ginger
2 garlic cloves

Method:

- Chop the onions and any whole apples you're using.
- Put everything in a large pan and stir to dissolve the sugar.

- Cook, stirring frequently, until it reaches the right consistency – for me this is just leaving a channel for a spoon.
- Place in sterilised jars and put the lids on while it's hot. Age for a month or so before eating.

Shrubs: Sweetened Drinking Vinegars

These sweetened drinking vinegars make excellent non-alcoholic aperitifs, and can be diluted with sparkling water, kombucha, ginger ale or tonic water. The principle is that fruit is macerated with sugar to extract the juice, which is then mixed with vinegar. The recipe works with all sorts of fruit: berries, drupes, tropicals and rhubarb. The choice of vinegar is entirely up to you, but 5 per cent acidity is best for preservation purposes. You can also add herbs and spices if you like. I prefer cold-steeping because I like the flavours better – and once you've tasted raw, sweetened rhubarb, there's really no other way! However, you can cook the fruit instead.

Ingredients:

2 cups of fruit
1 cup of sugar
1 cup of vinegar at 5 per cent

Cold prep method:

- Finely chop, grate or crush the fruit with the sugar.
- Cover and refrigerate, stirring daily.

Preparing a shrub. Sweetened raw rhubarb is delicious.

- When there is a pool of syrup, which will take about 24 hours, strain out the fruit (and eat with yoghurt!).
- Add the vinegar.
- Decant into a sterilised bottle.
- It is stable at room temperature, although the flavour will endure better long term in the fridge.

Hot prep method:
- Chop or mash the fruit.
- Place in a saucepan with the vinegar and sugar.
- Heat while stirring until the fruit has softened.
- Strain into a sterilised bottle using a sieve and funnel.
- Store as above.

Here are some other tried and tested combinations:

Peach and basil
Rhubarb
Strawberry
Pear and elderflower
Apple and ginger

SWITCHELS

The defining feature of switchels is the ginger they contain – you could use home-made ginger vinegar if you have some to hand, or any vinegar of your choice. This is best kept refrigerated, especially if you aren't sure of the acetic acid content of your vinegar, as its preservative qualities won't be as reliable. Drink switchels diluted 50/50 with sparkling water, kombucha or other mixers, in a glass filled with ice.

Ginger and Lemon switchel

For variation, swap the lemon for orange, and add a cinnamon stick.

Ingredients:
10cm piece of ginger
Juice and zest of one small lemon

Strawberry and ginger switchel – to be enjoyed in the garden.

400ml nutrient-rich vinegar
300ml raw honey or maple syrup

Method:
- Put everything in a jar and shake vigorously, or blend in a blender.
- Infuse for 24 hours.
- Strain and put in a sterilised bottle.
- Keep in the fridge for up to four weeks.

Another good combination uses strawberry (as shown in the picture), where I soaked about 100g of strawberries in some honey overnight, then strained that in, in place of the lemon juice.

OXYMELS

These functional mixtures contain raw honey and ACV, which extract bioactive phytochemicals from the herbal ingredients. I went to see Joanna Webster, a herbalist and fermenter based in Wells, to find out more.

Jo leaves her oxymels to mature for a month, during which time the osmotic action of the honey draws bioactive components out of the herbal elements of the oxymel, while the vinegar acts as a solvent. The flavours usually reach a maximum intensity after a month. Oxymels can have either specific functions, or general ones, depending upon their composition. Jo would recommend taking 10ml twice a day. She usually doesn't dilute them as this could also dilute their action on neural pathways via the tastebuds, but you can add to water if you prefer. Raw honey has a complex constitution and itself contains a myriad of bioactive components. Apple cider vinegar is often used as a solvent in oxymels – it is known to be a complex nutrient-rich vinegar. Jo firmly believes that oxymels are as delicious as they are beneficial – they can be used as drinking vinegars, and in cooking too.

Joanna Webster and her collection of oxymels.

General Oxymel Recipe
Ingredients:
This recipe is based on a 1:1:1 ratio.

½ cup raw honey
½ cup apple cider vinegar (5 per cent)
½ cup of herbs/flowers

Method:
- Mix raw honey with vinegar in a jug until dissolved.
- Place the chosen herbs in a sterilised jar.
- Pour the vinegar/honey mixture over the top and ensure there are no air bubbles.
- Store in a dark place for the osmotic and solvent action upon the herbal/floral/vegetal components to occur, shaking every couple of days.
- Taste after one month, strain and store in a glass jar.

Some popular and delicious preparations are listed below with their proposed benefits (*see* references for further information):

Lemon balm[31]	Calming/anti-anxiety.
Red clover[32]	Relieving menopause symptoms.
Lilac[33]	Anti-inflammatory.
Elderflower[34]	Influenza, bacterial sinusitis, bronchitis.
Rose[35]	Depression, grief, nervous stress and tension, allergies, headaches, migraine.
Chamomile[36]	Used to treat wounds, skin irritations, mouth and throat irritation.
Nettle[37]	Used for gout, to relieve muscle aches, and to minimise the symptoms of arthritis.
Dandelion flowers and roots[38]	Respiratory issues, mucus and phlegm, kidney, liver issues, stimulating digestion, nutrient absorption (the roots are rich in prebiotic inulin).

Fire Cider

Probably the best known oxymel is the age-old remedy fire cider, a combination of warming herbs and spices that will make you glow! The ingredients vary, but the recipe below gives a common combination. Fire cider can be used as a daily tonic, to be consumed diluted in water, or use it in cooking – add to rice, stir-fries, salad dressings, use as a marinade, or as a base for mayonnaise or dressing.

Ingredients:

1ltr ACV (or similar) – requires 5 per cent acidity unless refrigerated
50g horseradish, grated
1 chilli, sliced
50g ginger, grated
1 cinnamon stick
50g turmeric, grated
1tsp peppercorns
1 small lemon, sliced
1 small orange, sliced
½ small chopped onion
5 garlic cloves, grated
50g raw honey (optional)

Method:

- Place all the ingredients except the ACV and honey in a sterilised jar.
- Warm the apple cider vinegar, with the honey if using.
- Pour over the ingredients in the jar.
- Stir thoroughly to mix.
- Place parchment between a metal lid and the jar.
- Keep out of direct sunlight for four weeks, but give a daily shake.
- Strain.
- Store in a cool dark place, or refrigerate for up to six months. Gradually the activity and flavour of the ingredients will decrease.

COCKTAILS

Of course, your delicious home-made vinegars can be used to enhance alcoholic drinks too… here are some ideas.

The Pickleback Shot

This is a shot of (usually) whisky, swiftly followed by an equal shot of pickle-brine. As a fermenter, I would interpret this as being the salty lactic-acid juice of lactofermented cucumbers, but it actually means the sweetened liquor from vinegar pickles. Perhaps inspired by the traditional Russian pairing of vodka with pickles, the 2006 'invention' of this concept in New York has spread throughout the USA and Europe. Traditionally, the brine from pickled cucumbers is used for this – or alternatively, use some of your own diluted vinegar. Choose one with a sweetness to it, to balance the fiery, dry heat of the whisky. If it's 5 per cent acidity I would dilute one part vinegar to two parts water. Simply down the whisky, then immediately down the vinegar!

Aperitifs

The word 'aperitif' is derived from the Italian *aperitivo*, meaning 'appetiser', traditionally combining dry, tart and fizzy flavours imbibed to stimulate mouth and stomach before a meal. Knowing what we do about the influence of vinegar upon blood glucose levels (*see* page 156), this makes some sense, although including too much sugar would, of course, negate these effects.

Shrub Cocktails

Any home-made shrub can be used as a base for a delicious cocktail; as above, the combination of acidity and alcohol is a winner, but rhubarb and strawberry are particular favourites: try mixing one part shrub, with one part either tequila, gin or vodka over ice, topping with soda water and a sprig of mint.

Pimm's Cocktail

Interestingly, balsamic vinegar mixed with lemonade, with the addition of oranges, cucumber and mint, is an extremely convincing non-alcoholic substitute for Pimm's! It also acts as an enhancer for the usual and best loved Pimm's recipe (which is 1:3 ratio of Pimm's to lemonade or ginger beer), infused and served with quartered strawberries, cucumber, orange slices and mint. The addition of 1tbsp of balsamic vinegar (do substitute home-made Pedro-Ximinez vinegar, which is the most effective way of recreating a balsamic flavour in under three to twelve years!) per 100ml of Pimm's will elevate this to another level.

SALT AND VINEGAR POWDER – THE ELUSIVE DREAM

I have always wanted to re-create the salt and vinegar powder that gives crisps their inimitable appeal. Unfortunately it's harder than it looks, requiring the use of glacial acetic acid and sodium hydroxide. A patent has recently been granted for a new method,[39] so there's some fairly hardcore science involved. If you check the back of Britain's most popular salt and vinegar crisp, acetic acid is not even on the list of ingredients (it's malic and lactic acids).

A thick, balsamic-style vinegar reduction is similarly tricky to achieve: vinegar cannot be easily evaporated, nor concentrated by boiling. When water evaporates, so does acetic acid as their vapour pressures are very similar. The more heat that is applied, the worse the situation gets. The difference between the pressures is so slight that if you were to evaporate off several gallons of vinegar at room temperature, it would take years to concentrate it. If this sounds familiar, it's because this is how aged balsamic vinegar is made, but it takes constant topping up – twelve years and 18ltr to end up with 1ltr (see page 138)!

It is possible to create a salt of vinegar – sodium bi-acetate – by reacting vinegar with sodium bicarbonate, or dehydrating it on to maltodextrin powder, but home versions of these are poor relations to the crisp flavouring you will be seeking. Feel free to try, but don't blame me!

Boil 250ml of 5 per cent acidity vinegar with 30g baking powder, until the water has almost evaporated. Finish this off in the oven if you are using a saucepan you can't scrape, as you will need to scrape the dehydrated powder off the pan and into a pestle and mortar. Mix in half a teaspoon of sea salt – et voilà.

CHAPTER 17

VINEGAR FOR HEALTH – IS IT A SUPERFOOD?

Vinegar has been used as a remedy and disinfectant since the time of Hippocrates. This is firmly entrenched in folklore – for example, in the nursery rhyme of Jack and Jill, Jack's head is mended with vinegar and brown paper, which was in the olden days a popular remedy for bruising. Sheets of brown paper were soaked in hot vinegar, applied in layers over the affected area, and secured in place with a cloth or rag.

In the last century vinegar was overshadowed by pharmacological alternatives, and daily-shot enthusiasts were viewed with scepticism. But now vinegar is back in popular use, with research confirming that it has a range of pharmacological functions – nutrient rich, antioxidant, anti-inflammatory, anti-diabetic, anti-hypertensive, anti-hyperlipidic… there are even some clinical trials to back this up.

NUTRIENTS AND BIOACTIVE COMPONENTS IN VINEGAR

A double fermentation of a complex substrate such as apples or grains yields a vinegar rich in all kinds of bioactive components that can be useful to our bodies and microbiotas even in tiny quantities.[40] These include the following:

- Organic acids from the fermentation process: citric, tartaric, gluconic and lactic acids (though interestingly there are few recorded instances of gluconic and glucuronic acids in vinegars, which are major components of kombucha).
- Polyphenols: a wide-ranging group of important chemicals that serve as food for gut microbes and stimulators of various biological processes, for example antioxidant activity, blood-pressure control. These are chiefly derived from the raw starting materials: grains, fruit or vegetables. The anti-oxidant activity of the traditional balsamic vinegar of Modena was shown to increase with age, and recently, tomato vinegar has been shown to be a powerful anti-oxidant.
- Other nutrients include amino acids (often from the breakdown of microbes), GABA (the neurotransmitter gamma aminobutyric acid is found in brown rice vinegar), traces of various sugars, vitamins (mostly B3, B5, folic acid and C), and a variety of minerals.
- Flavour compounds: there are hundreds of these, including acetoin, esters and acetic acid.[41]

Vinegar and Blood Sugar Regulation

Type 2 diabetes is a preventable, chronic condition that affects how your body controls levels of circulating blood glucose, via the hormone insulin. Figures from 2022 show that over 7 per cent of the UK population are diabetic, with another 11 per cent potentially undiagnosed or prediabetic (at risk). Ten per cent of the entire NHS budget is spent on diabetic management and complications.[42]

When we eat starchy and sugary foods, enzymes in our mouth and guts readily break them down to easily absorbable glucose molecules. This can cause sudden 'spikes' in blood glucose. Our bodies respond by releasing similarly high amounts of insulin from the pancreas.

Insulin is a hormone that delivers glucose around the body: to cells for energy, to the liver or muscles to be stored as glycogen, to muscles to be used straightaway, or to be converted into fatty acids and stored as fat. When the glucose arrives at its destination, it is removed from the bloodstream.

Continual production of peaks of glucose and then of insulin can eventually lead to insulin resistance – the hormone stops doing its job properly, and levels of glucose circulating in the blood stay high. Long term this leads to the complications of type 2 diabetes, including heart disease, circulatory problems, chronic kidney disease, nerve damage, eye problems and depression.[43] The more starchy and sugary foods that you eat, the more likely you are eventually to face insulin resistance. Other factors, such as vitamin D deficiency, obesity and a sedentary lifestyle, do not help.

The Role of Vinegar

Although much in the news these days, the effect of vinegar on blood sugar levels has actually been researched for over a hundred years. Now enough evidence has been accrued to suggest that drinking a shot of diluted vinegar before a starchy meal could help to reduce glucose spikes by up to 30 per cent.[44, 45] Some of the effects are more marked in diabetic individuals than non-diabetics.

Vinegar is thought to reduce glucose spikes in the following ways:

- By temporarily inactivating alpha amylase, the enzyme in saliva that breaks down carbohydrates into glucose molecules. This means that glucose isn't processed until it reaches the gut, thus slowing glucose absorption and reducing subsequent spikes and insulin release.
- By travelling to our muscles, where it increases the rate of glycogen production, which in turn leads to more efficient uptake of glucose, so less insulin needs to be produced.[46]

Although I am neither diabetic nor pre-diabetic, I decided to investigate the vinegar/glucose spike story

Blood glucose responses to challenges with and without vinegar: days 1 and 2, white bread and butter without vinegar, and then with vinegar taken 10min before eating. Days 3 and 4, a scone, firstly without and the following day with vinegar 10min previously. An Abbott Freestyle Libre glucose monitor was used, and data produced using the Glucose Goddess app.

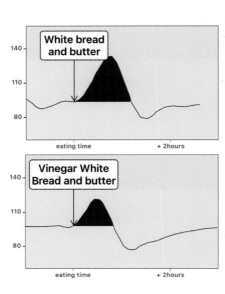

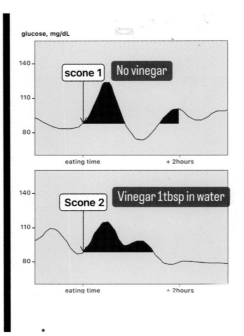

using a continuous glucose monitor (Abbot). The results show a clear vinegar effect, that I have repeatedly demonstrated. (Note that responses to glucose are individual and can be affected by what else you have eaten, drunk, done or felt, even the day before.)

I performed each experiment over two days, eating the food in question on an empty stomach at lunchtime.

A couple of diluted glasses of vinegar a day are not enough to single-handedly fully reverse or even prevent type 2 diabetes, but in conjunction with techniques including 'food combining' and 'clothing carbs',[43] it can probably help.

How To Do It

All edible vinegars work, but you will be delighted to learn that in one recent study, artisanal apple cider vinegar was found to be more effective in inhibiting alpha-amylase enzymes than an industrially produced one.[47] If you know the acidity of your vinegar, use 1tbsp of 5 per cent acetic acid. If it is a weaker scrap vinegar, add 2tbsp.

This unprepossessing little bottle of vinegar lives in my bag; I'll have 1tbsp diluted in sparkling water before a carb-fest.

Simply take a tablespoon of your favourite sugar-free vinegar (don't add extra sugar or you will lessen the glucose-spike lowering effect) and stir into a glass of sparkling or still water. You can drink this twenty minutes before, during, or even up to twenty minutes after your meal. This is a useful habit to get into before you're having a slice of cake for afternoon tea, or before a couple of biscuits for elevenses, or a pizza. You can use hot or cold water.

Alternatively use your favourite sugar-free vinegar to make a salad dressing (*see* page 150), and eat a dressed salad before every meal. The fibre in the vegetables will also help to slow down glucose absorption.

VINEGAR AND BLOOD LIPIDS

Cardiovascular disease is the leading cause of early mortality worldwide; treatment requires lifestyle modifications and a great many drugs. However, a daily dose of vinegar has been shown to have a positive effect on the lipid profile of diabetic study subjects, helping to reduce overall blood cholesterol and LDL, although the results were less clear in non-diabetics.

The mechanisms of how it works are not yet completely clear. Studies in mice have shown that acetic acid can inhibit enzymes involved in the synthesis of fatty acids and the formation of triglycerides in the liver, therefore reducing accumulation, which in turn can help lower blood lipid levels. It can also boost mechanisms that break down fats, helping to clear lipids from the blood.[48] Vinegar can also influence our DNA to encourage our mitochondria, the energy-consuming organelles in each of our cells, to burn more fat, especially in response to exercise.[49]

IMPORTANT: HOW TO TAKE/USE VINEGAR FOR HEALTH, SAFELY

When talking about vinegar other than as a condiment it's important to get some perspective. A little vinegar taken every day in conjunction with food and/or water is one thing, but overdoing it can have some unpleasant side effects – below are a few horror stories just to emphasise that moderation matters!

Vinegar and Teeth

Although the internet is full of advice regarding the use of white vinegar for tooth whitening and tartar removal (even a recent paper showed that vinegar, together with mechanical removal, was successful in reducing dental plaque and gingival inflammation),[50] there is as much evidence that although it can remove plaque it can also penetrate and break down the enamel on your teeth. This can lead to tooth sensitivity and damage. Here's how to benefit from your daily dose of vinegar, while keeping your teeth intact:

- Dilute your vinegar in water: 1tbsp of 5 per cent acetic acid in a glass of 200–300ml.
- Drink it with a straw to minimise exposure to your teeth.
- Avoid having your vinegar drink 20min before or after brushing your teeth. Brushing causes micro-abrasions in the enamel, and your teeth are vulnerable when brushed. Saliva has an important role in keeping teeth healthy and strong: it protects enamel by coating the teeth in calcium and other minerals. It also helps to neutralise acidic substances, so it is best to let it do its job.
- Have your vinegar with, or just before a meal, during the day when saliva production is at its greatest – not at night before you sleep.

Vinegar in Excess

You would have to try quite hard to physically damage yourself by sensibly including only a little extra vinegar in your diet, but there are cases where people have overdone it – drinking large quantities of undiluted vinegar can cause nausea, vomiting and indigestion. Oesophageal injuries have been reported,[51] and several cases of chemical burns from the use of neat apple cider vinegar to remove moles[52] – but the most extreme example has to be a young woman admitted to hospital with low blood potassium levels and osteoporosis: she had been consuming a cup (about 250ml) of apple cider vinegar a day for several years, and it was concluded that the excess acid had caused bone mineral leaching.[53]

Vinegar and Probiotics

The definition of a probiotic is 'live microorganisms that, when administered in adequate amounts, confer a health benefit on the host'.[54] Does vinegar contain probiotic microbes? You'd be forgiven for thinking not, and that oxygen-requiring AAB would not survive within the gut. There is, however, quite a lot of oxygen in our intestines, especially at the epithelium, so potentially they can survive, if not thrive.

Also, upon microbial examination of vinegars, and despite the fact that in the course of this book we focus on AAB as though they are the only microbes present, vinegars are usually full of all sorts of other bacteria, including many different species of AAB, *Lactobacillus* sp., and *Oenococcus* sp. A recent study found that an organic apple cider vinegar contained a wider variety of microbes than a non-organic one.[55] Generally, more variety of microbes is considered beneficial, because this will lead to greater diversity of biologically active end products.

The difficulty is that without a molecular biology lab, it is impossible to determine which microbes are present, so at best all we can say is that 'potentially vinegar *could* contain probiotic microbes'.

One AAB of particular interest is the vinegar isolate *Komagataeibacter xylinus*. It is highly acid tolerant and can survive the low oxygen environment of the gut, sequestering glucose and turning it into cellulose – in mice at any rate. Researchers propose to carry out further research in humans to see if this happens *in vivo*. If so, it could be added to the list of ways in which vinegar lowers blood glucose levels.[56]

CHAPTER 18

VINEGARS IN THE HOME

VINEGAR AS AN ANTISEPTIC AND A PRESERVATIVE

Acetic acid shows strong toxicity towards many pathogenic microbes. It behaves like a Trojan horse, sneaking inside first before orchestrating their death.

The reason it is so effective is because it is a weak acid. This is a confusing term unless you are a chemist; it doesn't mean that it's not a very good one, it means that in solution, it is mostly present as whole,

uncharged molecules of CH_3COOH, instead of being split into positive and negative ions like this: Ch_3COO^- and H^+. The extent to which this happens is influenced by the pH of the surroundings.

In an acidic environment it is mostly in CH_3COOH form. Because of the way microbial cell walls work, this whole molecule can get inside. Once there, something miraculous occurs: the cytoplasm has a high pH. The acetic-acid molecule dissociates into its CH_3COOH and H^+ parts, and when it does, it causes microbial havoc!

MECHANISM OF MICROBIAL DEATH

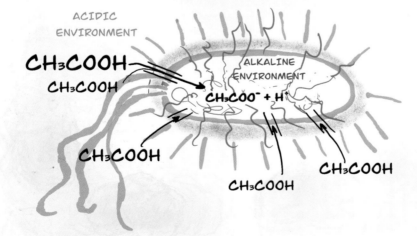

This picture illustrates the mode of action of acetic acid in vinegar upon microbes. At low pH, the undissociated molecule can enter the bacterial cell. In the more alkaline environment of the cell, it dissociates, and then causes all kinds of lethal reactions, resulting in microbial death.

It will acidify the cytoplasm and stop the cell from functioning, leading to its death.

At concentrations of 5 per cent, vinegar is extremely effective – this decreases with decreasing concentration, which is why 5 per cent acidity is so important.

WHY USE VINEGAR AS A CLEANING AGENT?

We are just beginning to realise the deleterious effects on health of a heavily ultra-processed food diet. It is further food for thought that our cleaning products contain chemicals that also could be doing us more harm than good. Have you ever choked at the overly strong smell of certain commercial cleaning products? General household cleaners can contain ammonia, ethylene glycol, monobutyl acetate, sodium hypochlorite (bleach) and anionic surfactants, while air fresheners contain formaldehyde, dichlorobenzene and petroleum distillates. As an alternative, you know where you are with vinegar, and you'll use far fewer plastic bottles and lose less money in the process.

What Type of Vinegar to Use

The best vinegars to use are the plain ones, of at least 5 per cent concentration, without clumps of mother and no residual sugar or you could end up with a sticky mess. The smell can be an issue for some people, but you can infuse your vinegar with saved citrus zest (just the zest as this contains little sugar) if this bothers you.

Xanthaclean is a firm fixture in my kitchen now. It is simply made by whisking xanthan gum and vinegar; its staying power makes it an excellent limescale remover, as evidenced by its effect on my shamefully scaly kettle!

As we have learned, vinegar does evaporate and you will soon get used to the smell!

Note: There's one important thing to note: while vinegar can be used in conjunction with other things for even better results, *NEVER mix it with BLEACH*. The reaction causes the release of toxic gas, which could be lethal in high volumes and unpleasant in lower ones.

Also, *vinegar isn't suitable for all surfaces* – do not use it regularly on marble or on polished slate, or on waxed wood, unless you specifically want to remove the wax, in which case it will do a good job! If in doubt, try a patch test first.

How To Use It

For windows: Vinegar alone applied sparingly to paper towel or a streak-free cloth will remove both water marks and smears. Alternatively put some in a labelled spray bottle and apply it directly.

Descaling the kettle: Fill the kettle with a couple of inches of vinegar, enough to cover the element if there is one, and boil. Leave to cool, then rinse.

Making a cleaning gel: Sometimes the problem with vinegar is it is just too runny. However, this problem is easy to solve. Mix one cup of vinegar with one level dessertspoon of xantham gum. Add a drop or two of lemon, or other essential oil if you prefer. Use a stick blender to mix this together, and store in a squeezy bottle for easy application. This is brilliant for limescale on taps where a little harder work is needed – leave for twenty minutes.

Note: If you've not used vinegar on any smart surface before, do a hidden patch test.

As an air freshener: It might sound strange, but vinegar spray for cleaning can also be used as an air freshener in a spray mister. The use of essential oils here will linger after the vinegar smell has gone – it dissipates quickly.

As a stainless-steel/ceramic hob cleaner: Vinegar is effective on its own, but you could use sodium bicarbonate powder with a little water first, and then add the vinegar – the effervescent action of the two together can help lift stubborn stains. Don't mix them together at the start, because after the fizzing stops, the bicarb will neutralise the vinegar, reducing its effectiveness. Ceramic hobs would do better with just vinegar, as bicarb can be quite abrasive with long-term use.

Minor drain blockages: Sprinkle 4tbsp baking soda followed by two cups of vinegar. This won't be as effective as sulphuric acid as found in drain cleaners, but is a good solution when drains are sluggish, and not completely blocked. Here the effervescent action of the two together can help dislodge a blockage.

Carpet stains: Half a cup of white vinegar mixed with 2tbsp salt is an effective carpet cleaner for stain removal. You can also add borax for more stubborn stains. Apply it, let it dry, and then vacuum the remaining residue. Check for colour-fastness first if it's a priceless Persian rug!

Weed killer: Neat vinegar will effectively kill weeds between paving slabs. Please throw away the glyphosate and try this instead. Mix approximately 50g salt with 1ltr of 10 per cent vinegar and a squeeze of Fairy Liquid. Mix well and spray where needed. Repeat frequently as it won't be harmful for pets or children once dry.

As a moth killer: The eggs of those horrible little house moths that eat carpets, clothes and furniture do not much like 5 per cent white vinegar. Spray in their hiding places in March, and with any luck they won't hatch out in April or May. Patch test any delicate fabrics first!

Antiseptic 'magic' spray: This foodsafe spray is the wonder product of the fermentation world – many members of the Fermenter's Guild UK swear by it. No one can remember who invented it – it certainly wasn't me, but it's a most effective non-ammonia-based, food-safe antibacterial spray that can be used on most surfaces, and for cleaning fermentation vessels before use.

Simply mix together the following ingredients in a jug:

250ml vodka
250ml 5 per cent vinegar
50g salt
and place in a labelled spray bottle.

Antiseptic wipes: The following is another way of using 'magic spray', with reusable bamboo wipes. You will need a packet of bamboo wipes, and a glass Kilner jar that is taller than the wipes, or a baby-wipes box.

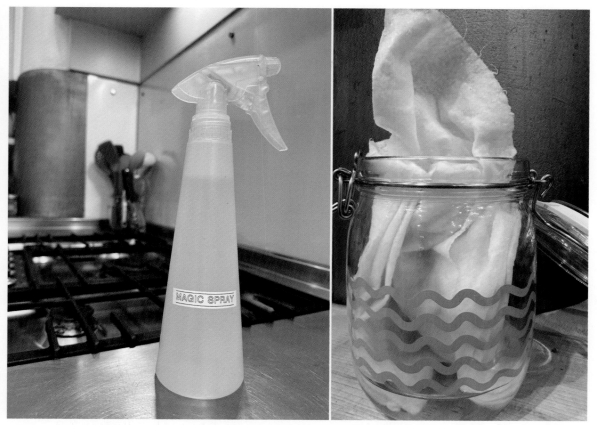

Another permanent fixture: magic spray and wipes are an economical and sustainable alternative to commercial cleaners.

Method:

- Place a quantity of magic spray in a flat tub.
- Place a packet of bamboo reusable wipes into the liquid and let them absorb it. Interweave the pieces of cloth (there's a knack to it – watch the YouTube video *My Green Nest, cloth wipes from fold to pop* to help you).
- Roll them up and place them inside the jar, with a couple of inches of magic spray at the bottom.
- Wipes can be used, washed and resoaked.

VINEGAR FOR FUN

There are some irresistible kitchen-based experiments that can be carried out using vinegar, which are perfect entertainment for both children and adults.

RED CABBAGE AND VINEGAR

Observe the effect of pH on red cabbage: red cabbage gets its colour from a compound called cyanidin. This is an anthocyanin, which is sensitive to changes in pH – when more or less H^+ is present, the structure of the molecule changes, and this is enough to alter the wavelengths of light reflected by the compound.

Instructions:

- Grate about three tablespoonfuls of raw red cabbage into a heat-proof bowl and add about 50ml hot water.
- Strain off the resulting juice, and stir fry the cabbage for your next meal. It will be a dark bluey purple.
- Mix 100ml of vinegar with a heaped tablespoon of cornflour (this helps the patterns to last longer).
- Using a dropper or a teaspoon, carefully add some of the purple juice. Where the acid meets the indicator, a beautiful vivid magenta will result.

VINEGAR AND AN EGG

Vinegar can dissolve calcium carbonate, which is the major component of eggshells. Place an egg in vinegar and leave it undisturbed for 48 hours. When you examine it, you will find that the shell has completely dissolved, leaving the inner membrane intact, and you will be able to see the yolk, and even

The pH indicator qualities of red cabbage.

Don't press too hard! Without its protective shell, the inner membrane will soon give way and there will be raw egg everywhere.

roll it about in your hand. It will swell up massively. You can then poach and eat it (but don't leave it too long – it is only edible within 48 hours).

VOLCANO ERUPTION

Sodium bicarbonate, vinegar and orange food colouring can make a spectacular display of lava – which is even more impressive if you've made a papier-mâché volcano first. The sodium bicarbonate reacts with the vinegar to release massive amounts of CO_2.

MAKE A RAINBOW!

Vinegar is commonly found in hues of orange, rust, red or dark brown. Since I discovered that the bright blue phycocyanin pigment produced by the blue-green alga *Spirulina* is heat stable, I've been able to make a whole rainbow of colours! It also lasts for weeks without breaking down, so now you can use a white-wine vinegar as a base to make a green one, while for a pure blue one, water kefir vinegar, cucumber or distilled will give you the best colour. Incidentally, this blue pigment is rich in antioxidants too.

Make your very own volcanic eruption! Bicarbonate of soda and vinegar, with a little food colouring atop a papier-maché mountain. I put clingfilm over the top so that the mountain could be reused.

The acid stable nature of the phycocyanin pigment means that fun can be had with a rainbow of vinegars!

A SUMMARY OF THE DOS AND DON'TS OF VINEGAR MAKING

- Try everything! Vinegar making is a safe DIY activity, and the worst that can happen is that you decide to discard it.
- Remember to acidify vegetable juices that you are making wine from to ensure good alcoholic fermentation.
- Storage matters, and too much oxygen can ruin a perfectly good vinegar.
- Ageing can have a profound difference on the flavours – usually good.
- Make sure everything is clean before you start.
- Use good quality fruit and vegetables.
- Don't be put off if your first batch isn't delicious. Just like sourdough, it might take a couple of attempts to get into the swing of things. Start simply: follow the recipe on page 45.
- Don't worry if you have kahm yeast on the top – it happens to us all.
- Don't use vinegars for long-term pickling or selling without checking the acidity (*see* page 69) – instead, refrigerate and keep for a fortnight.

PRODUCING VINEGAR FOR BUSINESS

WHAT YOU NEED TO KNOW ABOUT THE LAW

Trading Standards Vinegar Recommendation

If you are planning to sell vinegar, you will need to meet certain trading standards criteria: although there is no 'legal' definition of vinegar, there is a British Standard BSEN13188:2000 which is 'persuasive'. Acetic acid levels below the 'Standard' value of 5 per cent weight/volume for fruit vinegars, beer, mead or cider vinegars, or 6 per cent for wine vinegar, would most likely not be acceptable. Do talk to your local trading standards representative for more information.

Hazard Analysis and Critical Control Points (HACCP)

To produce vinegar commercially, you will need to provide detailed information for your local council's Environmental Health Department, to show that you have considered every aspect of your production: where things could go wrong, and how to produce a high quality, safe product. Further information is available at www.gov.uk/food-safety-hazard-analysis.

Distillation Licence

To sell vinegar, you will need to measure accurately the residual alcohol content, which will need to be 0.5 per cent abv or below. As we have seen, choices are limited to expensive equipment, sending away for analysis or distillation. To use a still for alcohol production requires a licence, but it's difficult to get approval – my own application to run a still for diagnostic purposes was turned down. If you do want to give home distillation a go, you will need to fill in an application for a licence to carry on an excise trade. You can find out more information by visiting www.gov.uk and searching for form L5.

Growing Vinegar Mothers for Friends or for Selling

Nothing is more satisfying than a round, flat, pale, shiny disc of vinegar mother, even though they aren't strictly necessary. To grow them specifically, I suggest a couple of changes to the regular surface method. The production of cellulose requires sugar, so be sure to include some extra in your acetic fermentation. There is always an expectation that a vinegar mother will be round – so as not to disappoint, use round vessels that are neither too shallow, nor too wide, with a depth of 20cm and a diameter of about 8cm. Incubation at 28°C will offer the most successful environment for growth, and covering with cloth is a good idea to reduce any condensation dripping back on to the mother and preventing its rapid development. Don't disturb the mothers, and harvest them when they are 1cm thick. If posting, use a sealed sachet, and always include at least 200ml of liquid mother as well.

REFERENCES

[1] Grand View Research. Acetic Acid Market. https://www.grandviewresearch.com/industry-analysis/acetic-acid-market.

[2] Chem Europe. Chem Europe. *Acetic Acid data* https://www.chemeurope.com/en/encyclopedia/Acetic_acid.html.

[3] KAT *V*. DIMENT. *R.P.C.* **67**, 158–163 (1950).

[4] Martin Adams and Tim R. Smith in *London's Industrial Archaeology* **10**, 15–22.

[5] Jabłońska, J. and Tawfik, D. S. 'The evolution of oxygen-utilizing enzymes suggests early biosphere oxygenation', *Nat Ecol Evol* **5**, 442–448 (2021).

[6] Katsaros,T., Liritzis, I. and Laskaris, N. Identification of Theophrastus' pigments egyptios yanos and psimython from archaeological excavations, *ArcheoSciences*, **34** | 2010, 69–80.

[7] Smith, R., *Vinegar: The Eternal Condiment*, Southport, North Carolina Spikehorn Press (2020).

[8] Bourgeois, J. and Barja, F. (2009). The history of vinegar and of its acetification systems. *Archives des Sciences* **62**, 147–160

[9] China Daily. Vinegar Culture in China. https://usa.chinadaily.com.cn/culture/2011-03-24/content_12222808.htm#:~:text=As%20a%20story%20goes%2C%20a,stored%20them%20in%20a%20jar.

[10] Rossella Lorenzi, 'Cleopatra pearl cocktail proven possible', nbcnews.com/id/wbna 38536846

[11] 'Never Thirsty. Why was wine or sour vinegar given to Christ on the cross?' www.neverthirsty.org/bible-qa/qa-archives/question/why-did-they-give-wine-vinegarsour-wine-to-those-who-were-hung-on-the-cross/.

[12] Go East [date unknown] https://goeastmandarin.com/why-does-drink-vinegar-mean-jealous-in-chinese/ [accessed online 15/5/23].

[13] Pfeiffer, T. and Morley, A. 'An evolutionary perspective on the Crabtree effect' *Front Mol Biosci* **1**, 17 (2014).

[14] Nakano, S., Fukaya, M. and Horinouchi, S. 'Putative ABC transporter responsible for acetic acid resistance in Acetobacter aceti', *Appl Environ Microbiol* **72**, 497–505 (2006).

[15] Xie, Z. *et al.* 'Vinegar Volatile Organic Compounds: Analytical Methods, Constituents, and Formation Processes', *Front. Microbiol.* **13**, 907883 (2022).

[16] Yasmin, S. *et al.* 'Outbreak of Botulism after Consumption of Illicit Prison-Brewed Alcohol in a Maximum Security Prison – Arizona, 2012', *J Correct Health Care* **21**, 327–334 (2015).

[17] Sharafi, S., Rasooli, I. and Beheshti-Maal, K. Isolation, characterization and optimization of indigenous acetic acid bacteria and evaluation of their preservation methods. *Iran J Microbiol.* 2010 Mar;2(1):38–45

[18] Adams, M. R. and Twiddy, D. R. 'Performance parameters in the quick vinegar process', *Enzyme and Microbial Technology* **9**, 369–373 (1987).

[19] Lim, J.-M. *et al.* 'Significance of LED lights in enhancing the production of vinegar using Acetobacter pasteurianus AP01', *Prep Biochem Biotechnol* **52**, 38–47 (2022).

[20] Malle, B. *The artisanal vinegar maker's handbook: crafting quality vinegars - fermenting, distilling, infusing* (Spikehorn Press, 2015).

[21] Wassermann, B., Müller, H. and Berg, G. 'An Apple a Day: Which Bacteria Do We Eat With Organic and Conventional Apples?' *Front Microbiol* **10**, 1629 (2019).

[22] The Food Standards Agency 'My HACCP – Patulin', https://myhaccp.food.gov.uk/sites/default/files/2022-05/factsheet_patulin.docx.

[23] Góral, I. and Wojciechowski, K. 'Surface activity and foaming properties of saponin-rich plants extracts', *Advances in Colloid and Interface Science* **279**, 102145 (2020).

[24] Redzepi, R. and Zilber, D. *The Noma guide to fermentation: foundations of flavor* (Artisan, 2018).

[25] Tomar, O., Akarca, G. and Çağlar, A. 'Physicochemical, Microbiological and Sensory Properties of Red Beet Vinegar', *Pamukkale J Eng Sci* **26**, 1234–1238 (2020).

[26] Arachchige Buddhika Niroshie Perumpuli, P., Mirihana A. M. and Nidarhsa Kaumal, M. 'Production of Antioxidant Rich Tomato Vinegar: An Alternative to Coconut Vinegar in Culinary Production', *Curr. Appl. Sci. Technol.* **22**, (2021).

[27] Escobar Rodríguez, C. *et al.* 'The Bacterial Microbiome of the Tomato Fruit is Highly Dependent on the Cultivation Approach and Correlates with Flavor Chemistry', *Front Plant Sci* **12**, 775722 (2021).

[28] Kurahashi, A. 'Ingredients, Functionality, and Safety of the Japanese Traditional Sweet Drink Amazake', *J Fungi (Basel)* **7**, 469 (2021).

[29] Nabubuya, A. *et al.* 'Viscoelastic properties of sweet potato complementary porridges as influenced by endogenous amylases', *Food Sci Nutr* **5**, 1072–1078 (2017).

[30] Monaco, F. (2020). Salsamenta: a recipe for Columella's Fig Vinegar. Available at https://tavolamediterranea.com/2018/09/06/columellas-fig-vinegar/ [Accessed March 2023].

[31] Scholey, A. *et al.* 'Anti-Stress Effects of Lemon Balm-Containing Foods', *Nutrients* **6**, 4805–4821 (2014).

[32] Kanadys, W. *et al.* 'Evaluation of Clinical Meaningfulness of Red Clover (*Trifolium pratense* L.) Extract to Relieve Hot Flushes and Menopausal Symptoms in Peri- and Post-Menopausal Women: A Systematic Review and Meta-Analysis of Randomized Controlled Trials', *Nutrients* **13**, 1258 (2021).

[33] Woźniak, M., Michalak, B., Wyszomierska, J., Dudek, M. K. and Kiss, A. K. 'Effects of Phytochemically Characterized Extracts From *Syringa vulgaris* and Isolated Secoiridoids on Mediators of Inflammation in a Human Neutrophil Model', *Front. Pharmacol.* **9**, 349 (2018).

[34] Ulbricht, C. *et al.* 'An Evidence-Based Systematic Review of Elderberry and Elderflower (*Sambucus nigra*) by the Natural Standard Research Collaboration', *Journal of Dietary Supplements* **11**, 80–120 (2014).

[35] Boskabady, M. H., Shafei, M. N., Saberi, Z. and Amini, S. 'Pharmacological effects of rosa damascena', *Iran J Basic Med Sci* **14**, 295–307 (2011).

[36] Gupta. 'Chamomile: A herbal medicine of the past with a bright future' (review), *Mol Med Rep* **3**, (2010).

[37] Bhusal, K. K. *et al.* 'Nutritional and pharmacological importance of stinging nettle (*Urtica dioica* L.): A review', *Heliyon* **8**, e09717 (2022).

[38] Olas, B. 'New Perspectives on the Effect of Dandelion, Its Food Products and Other Preparations on the Cardiovascular System and Its Diseases', *Nutrients* **14**, 1350 (2022).

[39] 'Preparation of a Powdered Vinegar' (2020). European patent no. EP 3 115 448 A1

[40] Chen, G.-L. *et al.* 'Vinegar: A potential source of healthy and functional food with special reference to sugarcane vinegar', *Front Nutr* **10**, 1145862 (2023).

[41] Xia, T., Zhang, B., Duan, W., Zhang, J. and Wang, M. 'Nutrients and bioactive components from vinegar: A fermented and functional food', *Journal of Functional Foods* **64**, 103681 (2020).

[42] NHS UK, Diabetes Data. www.england.nhs.uk/statistics/statistical-work-areas/integrated-performance-measures-monitoring/diabetes-data/.

[43] Inchauspé, J. *Glucose revolution: the life-changing power of balancing your blood sugar* (Short Books, 2022).

[44] Siddiqui, F. J. *et al.* 'Diabetes Control: Is Vinegar a Promising Candidate to Help Achieve Targets?' *J Evid Based Integr Med* **23**, 2156587217753004 (2018).

[45] Ceriello, A. *et al.* 'HbA1c variability predicts cardiovascular complications in type 2 diabetes regardless of being a glycemic target', *Cardiovasc Diabetol* **21**, 13 (2022).

[46] Mitrou, P. *et al*. 'Vinegar Consumption Increases Insulin-Stimulated Glucose Uptake by the Forearm Muscle in Humans with Type 2 Diabetes', *J Diabetes Res* **2015**, 175204 (2015).

[47] Ousaaid, D. *et al*. 'The Nutritional and Antioxidant Potential of Artisanal and Industrial Apple Vinegars and Their Ability to Inhibit Key Enzymes Related to Type 2 Diabetes In Vitro.' *Molecules* **27**, 567 (2022).

[48] Seo, K.-I. *et al*. 'Anti-obesity and anti-insulin resistance effects of tomato vinegar beverage in diet-induced obese mice', *Food Funct.* **5**, 1579 (2014).

[49] Santos, H. O., de Moraes, W. M. A. M., da Silva, G. A. R., Prestes, J. and Schoenfeld, B. J. 'Vinegar (acetic acid) intake on glucose metabolism: A narrative review', *Clinical Nutrition ESPEN* **32**, 1–7 (2019).

[50] Asaad, N. and Laflouf, M. 'Effectiveness of Apple Cider Vinegar and Mechanical Removal on Dental Plaque and Gingival Inflammation of Children with Cerebral Palsy', *Cureus* **14**, e26874 (2022).

[51] Chang, J., Han, S. E., Paik, S. S. and Kim, Y. J. 'Corrosive Esophageal Injury due to a Commercial Vinegar Beverage in an Adolescent', *Clin Endosc* **53**, 366–369 (2020).

[52] Feldstein, S., Afshar, M. and Krakowski, A. C. 'Chemical Burn from Vinegar Following an Internet-based Protocol for Self-removal of Nevi', *J Clin Aesthet Dermatol* **8**, 50 (2015).

[53] Lhotta, K., Höfle, G., Gasser, R. and Finkenstedt, G. 'Hypokalemia, hyperreninemia and osteoporosis in a patient ingesting large amounts of cider vinegar', *Nephron* **80**, 242–243 (1998).

[54] Hill, C. *et al*. 'The International Scientific Association for Probiotics and Prebiotics consensus statement on the scope and appropriate use of the term probiotic.' *Nat Rev Gastroenterol Hepatol* **11**, 506–514 (2014).

[55] Trček, J., Mahnič, A. and Rupnik, M. 'Diversity of the microbiota involved in wine and organic apple cider submerged vinegar production as revealed by DHPLC analysis and next-generation sequencing', *International Journal of Food Microbiology* **223**, 57–62 (2016).

[56] Lavasani, P. S., Motevaseli, E., Sanikhani, N. S. and Modarressi, M. H. 'Komagataeibacter xylinus as a novel probiotic candidate with high glucose conversion rate properties', *Heliyon* **5**, e01571 (2019).

GLOSSARY

acetification The process of turning an alcohol base into vinegar.

antioxidant A substance that protects cells from damage caused by unstable molecules called free radicals.

Brix A measure of dissolved sugars (and other solids) in an aqueous solution, determined by differences in refractive indices between distilled water and the test sample.

cultivar A type of a particular plant that has been selected for certain traits. Upon propagation the traits are retained.

drupes Stone fruits.

equivalence point The point in a titration where the amount of titrant completely neutralises the test solution.

eukaryote Single or multicellular organisms whose cells contain a nucleus and sophisticated membrane-bound organelles.

genus or **genera** A collection of species grouped together based on various similarities.

gram negative/positive Classification of bacteria according to their reaction to the gram stain test. Microbes with a thick peptidoglycan layer are 'gram positive' (for example *Lactobacillus* sp.); microbes lacking this are gram negative (for example AAB). It is often used in describing microbes, and was essential in their identification before the advent of molecular genetics.

kombucha A drink produced by fermenting sweetened tea with a SCOBY.

lees The sediment, or dregs, that settle in the bottom of a fermentation vessel, comprising dead yeast cells, fragments of pulp, and the insoluble end products of metabolism.

malo-lactic fermentation When a strain of lactic acid bacteria starts to ferment in a finished grape wine, or unfinished vinegar. Carbon dioxide is produced.

meniscus The curve seen at the surface when liquids are placed in a container. It is more visible in narrow tubes – in titration, we read the scale at the bottom of the meniscus.

molarity The number of moles of a substance dissolved in 1 litre of solution.

mole The amount of substance that contains 6.02×10^{23} particles. It is used in chemistry for comparing quantities of different compounds.

must The prepared juice or pulp for fermenting to wine.

pomace The solid remains of fruit or vegetable matter after pressing for juice, containing skins, pulp, seeds, stems.

prokaryote A simple, single-cellular organism lacking a nucleus and other organelles.

racking Moving wine (or in our case, also vinegar) from the lees by transferring it to a fresh vessel.

SCOBY A symbiotic culture of bacteria and yeast – it may exist as a cellulose mat.

species A microbial species is a group of strains that can exchange genetic material, but is less likely to do so with others.

strain A subtype of a microbial species that has specific characteristics and is genetically distinct.

symbiosis A close, long-term biological interaction between different species.

titration A method of analysis using a chemical equation and a known amount of one substance to determine the amount of an unknown substance.

water kefir A drink made from water kefir grains, a type of SCOBY.

LIST OF SUPPLIERS

The simplicity of vinegar manufacture means that few specific pieces of equipment are needed – and those that are, are readily available through a quick internet search. A few more specific items are listed below.

Artisan Vinegars
The Slow Vinegar Company –
www.theslowvinegarcompany.co.uk

Bread Proofer
www.brodandtaylor.uk

Chemical Reagents
APC Pure: www.APC.com

Glucose Monitor
Abbott – www.freestyle.abbott

pH meters
Apera Instruments PH20 Value pH Meter available at www.osmotics.co.uk
   Hi-98118 Groline Waterproof pH Meter available at www.hannainstruments.co.uk

Rice Koji
The Koji Kitchen: www.thekojikitchen.com
Umami Chef: www.umami-chef.co.uk

FURTHER READING

There are many other excellent texts about vinegar; here are a few of them:

Baudar, P. *Wildcrafted Vinegars: Making and Using Unique Acetic Acid Ferments for Quick Pickles, Hot Sauces, Soups, Salad Dressings, Pastes, Mustards, and More* (2023), White River Junction, USA: Chelsea Green.

Clutton, A. *The Vinegar Cupboard: Recipes and History of an Everyday Ingredient* (2019), London, UK: Bloomsbury Absolute.

Diacono, M. *Sour: The Magical Element that Transforms your Cooking* (2019), London: Quadrille Publishing.

Katz, S.E. *Sandor Katz's Fermentation Journeys: Recipes, Techniques and Traditions from Around the World* (2021), White River Junction, Vermont: Chelsea Green Publishing.

Malle, B. and Schmickl, H. *The Artisanal Vinegar Maker's Handbook: Crafting Quality Vinegars – Fermenting, Distilling, Infusing* (2015), English edition. Austin, Texas: Spikehorn Press.

Redzepi, R. and Zilber, D. *The Noma Guide to Fermentation: Foundations of Flavor* (2018), New York: Artisan (Foundations of Flavor).

Shockey, K. *Homebrewed Vinegar: How to Ferment 60 Delicious Varieties: Including Carrot-Ginger, Beet, Brown Banana, Pineapple, Corncob, Honey, and Apple Cider Vinegar* (2021), North Adams, MA: Storey Publishing.

Smith, R. *Vinegar: The Eternal Condiment* (2020), Southport, North Carolina: Spikehorn Press.

Turkell, M. H. *Acid trip: travels in the world of vinegar: with recipes from leading chefs, insights from top producers, and step-by-step instructions on how to make your own* (2017), New York, NY: Abrams.

INDEX

acetabulum 12
acetator 17
acetic acid
    characteristics 8
    chemical formula 8
    formation from alcohol 25
    glacial 8
    industrial production of 8
    isolation of 8
acetic acid bacteria (AAB)
    classification 23
    desirable attributes 27
    energy sources 25
    evolution 10
    oxidation pathway 25
    structure 23
    temperature 23
acetifiers
    industrial 15–17
air pump generator 53
    home Boerhaave method 50
    home generator 52
    home surface method 49
acidity
    percentage 73, 76
    troubleshooting 76–79
airlock 36
alchemy 9
alcohol
alcohol bases 107
alcohol detection 74–75
alegar 8, 85
all-in-one vinegars 44, 125–133
amazake 122
amino acids 8, 65, 103, 108
ancient Greece 13
ancient Islamic civilisation 13
ancient Rome 13
Andalusia 140
antioxidant 115,119,165
antiseptic 160, 163
antiseptic spray 160,162
apple cider vinegar
apple cider vinegar (raw) 14, 27
Archimedes 99
Aspall 14, 45
Aspergillus oryzae 121
attenuation 104
    juice 113
    pulp 113
    scrap 131

Babylonians 11
balsamic vinegar of Modena 138–139,
    156
barley 85, 122, 140, 142
beer 85, 49
beetroot 23, 71, 115
blackberries 116
blood sugar 148,156–7, 169
Boerhaave home set-up 50
Boerhaave method 16

Boerhaave, Herman 16
bottling 66
brix 100

cabbage, red 164
calcium carbonate 18,19
Campden tablets 109
carbon dioxide 25, 36, 66, 73
cells 21,23
cellulase 23
cellulose
    bacterial production of 10, 15,
        24–28
    industrial production of 24
chamomile 153
chaptalisation 97
cholesterol 158
chutney (fruit pulp recipe) 151
cider 49
citrus 86–87, 119, 161
cleaning 41–42
Cleopatra 18
Clostridium botulinum 32
cloth cover 36
cocktails 154
Columella, Lucius 12, 138, 169
contamination 79–81, 109–110
continuous culture 29, 83
Crabtree effect 22
crema di aceto 144
cucumber vinegar 88
Cyanobacteria 10

damsons 117
dandelion 153
dates 12, 59, 129
density 73, 74, 101
dental health 159
distillation 143
distilled vinegar 143

eels 81
eggs
    poached 137
    dissolving shell 164
elderflower 119,133,145,153
    alcohol base 119
    oxymel 153
enrichment 96–98
enzymes
    alcohol dehydrogenase 25
    aldehyde dehydrogenase 25
    amylase 97, 122–123, 157
    invertase 22
    saccharification 97, 122–124, 140
esters 31, 82, 156
estimating 96, 102,
ethanol 23–25, 73, 101
eukaryotes 10,22
evaporation 15, 18, 26, 36, 50, 59 , 77

fermentation 89

overview of pathway 20
    primary 106
    reasons for 30–31
    secondary 106
fermentation box 50
fig vinegar 12, 126
filtering 63
fining 64
fire cider 154
fizzy vinegar 78
flavour 41, 48, 56, 64, 135
flocculation 104
flowers 145
foam 94
food safety 32
four thieves vinegar 146
freezing 49
fructose 22
fruit flies 80
fruit preparation 89–95

garlic 145, 148, 149, 151, 154
ginger
    alcohol base 120
    quick pickles 148
    switchel 151
glassware 34
glucose 22,23
grape must 12–13, 138
grapes 114
Guild of Fermenters 132, 162

halal 13
Hannibal 19
Hazard Analysis and Critical Control
    Points (HACCP) 167
health 32, 156–162
Heita, son of Du Kang 18
herbs 146
Hippocrates 13, 156
honey 11, 145, 152, 153,
hydrogen peroxide 47
hydrometer 98–101

Ibn Hayyan, Jabir 9
incubator 39–40
industrialisation 17, 26
infusion 144, 146
insulin 156–157
invertase 22
Italy 138

Japan 122
jealousy 19
Jerez 15, 79, 140–1
juicer 93
juicing 91–94

kahm yeast 41, 78, 79–80
kefir 10, 124, 136, 172
koji 97, 121–123, 134
kombucha 10, 23, 28, 118

lactic acid bacteria 115, 171
lead poisoning 13
lees 37,38, 108
lemon balm 153
light 59
lilac 153
limoncello vinegar 86
liquid vinegar starter 26, 55, 57

magic spray 163
malolactic fermentation 78
malt vinegar 141
malting process 142
Marmite 20
Martin Pouret 13
micronutrients 156
mother of vinegar 10,14,23, 25, 84
    characteristics 25
    comparison with SCOBY 28
    grow your own 26
    growth 28
    storage 29
mould 81
Mycoderma aceti 26

Neolithic period 11
nettle 153
non-brewed condiment 9
nutrients 59, 105

oats 122
onions, pickled red 150
optimisation of 58
organic vegetables 90
Orléans 13
Orléans method 13, 15
over-oxidation 45
oxidation 47
oxygen 8, 10, 25, 73, 106
oxymel 13,145, 152–153

Pasteur, Louis 21,23
pasteurisation 21, 64, 82, 97, 108
peaches 117
pears 114
pectinase 109
Pedro Ximinez vinegar 86
persimmon vinegar 127–128
pH
    difference from titratable acidity 68
    for AAB growth 23
    optimisation of 58
pH meter 67
    scale 68
Pickleback Shot 154
pickles
    daikon radish quick pickle 148
    dill pickled beetroot 149
    pickled courgettes 148
    pink pickled onions 150
    quick pickled magnolia blossoms 149
pickling 144, 147–150
pineapple vinegar 131–132
plague 138

plum vinegar 117
    crema di aceto di prugna 147
pomegranate vinegar 87
posca 12, 19
potential acidity 60
prokaryotes 10, 23
protected designation of origin (PDO) 138
protein 137

qu 140
quick pickling 148
quince 114

raisin vinegar 129
ready-made juice alcohol base 120
record keeping 38
red clover 153
red wine 47, 48, 115
refractometry 100
respiration 22
rice vinegar 122
Roman empire 12
rose 153

saccharification 121
sake 134
salad dressing 150
salt and vinegar powder 155
sapa 12
Sarson's vinegar 14
SCOBY 10
sherry vinegar 139
shrubs 144, 151
siphon 36
sodium bicarbonate 165, 162
solera 139, 141
sour 135, 136
spirit vinegar 86, 143
stepwise fermentation 61
sterols 22
storage
    of mother of vinegar 29
    of vinegar 64, 66
stuck fermentation 77
submerged fermentation 17
sucrose 22
sugar 28, 103
    amount for alcohol fermentation 96
    in vinegar 28
    type 102
sulphites 47
sulphuric acid 47
surface method 49
sweet potato 123
switchel 144,151

Tang dynasty 19
tarragon 145
taste receptors 135
teeth 159
temperature
    for acetifiation 58
    for alcohol bases 103
    for all-in-ones 126

    for pasteurisation 64
titration, acid-base 69
    calculations for titration 73
    difference from pH 68
    of coloured vinegar 71
tomatoes 119–120
trading standards 73, 167
tradition
trickly 16
two-stage vinegar 44,45

vinaigrier 35
vinegar
    ageing 64
    antioxidant activity 156
    basic (rudimentary) recipe 45
    blood lipids 158
    blood sugar regulation 156–158
    cleaning agent 161–163
    definition of 7
    drinking vinegar 147, 158
    endpoint of fermentation 62
    etymology 8
    in excess 159
    methods of making 44
    monitoring of acetification 67
    nutrition 156
    odours 82
    optimisation of acetification 58–67
    probiotics 159
    signs of acetification 62
    stages in production 46
    storing vinegar 66
    taste 135
vinegar eels 81
vinegar starter 24
    acquiring a starter 26
    addition of starter 56
    calculations for addition of starter 57
    liquid vs solid 25, 56
    maintaining flavour 57
    maintenance of 29
vodka 86, 87

water kefir 124
wine thief 38, 100
wine vinegar 48–49
wood chips 65, 133
wood wool 17, 51, 141
wooden barrel 35

xanthan gum 161

yeast
    alcohol production 10,21
    baker's 21
    brewers 21
    characteristics 22
    discovery of 21
    evolution 10
    structure 21
yeast nutrient 88, 108-9

zhenjiang black vinegar 140–141

First published in 2024 by
The Crowood Press Ltd
Ramsbury, Marlborough
Wiltshire SN8 2HR

enquiries@crowood.com

www.crowood.com

British Library Cataloguing-in-Publication Data
A catalogue record for this book is available from the British
Library.

ISBN 978 0 7198 4366 2

Typeset by Envisage IT
Cover design by Nick May/www.bluegecko22.com
Printed and bound in India by Nutech Publishing Services

Wine and the Sun will make vinegar without any shout-
ing to help them

George Eliot

DEDICATION

For my dear Papa.

ACKNOWLEDGEMENTS

At first it seemed a daunting task to write on vinegar when
there are so many well-respected titles already in print, but
it soon became clear that the subject is so fascinating that
there is an infinite amount to say about it! As I come to the
end of this project, I find myself quite obsessed: I have six new
vinegars on the go, and around twenty that I am struggling to
part with, though should probably bestow upon the following
colleagues, friends and family who have been indispensable
in helping me to put this book together.

First I must thank Joanna Webster for invaluable insights
into making oxymels and for letting me help with the ACV
making last year; it was enormous fun! Then Debbie Guthrie
for helping me to remember my A-level chemistry when it
came to titration calculations, and David McKeith for some
extra maths help. Jane and Paul MacFarlane for the generous
donation of tens of kilos of apples for me to play with; Kathryn
Ashmore for her top-class photography skills; Xanthe Clay
for letting me go on and on about vinegar, and for giving me
access to her wood-chip collection; and the myriad members
of the Fermenters' Guild for coming through and answering
some tricky questions – also everyone on Instagram who took
part in the 'What is vinegar?' polls.

Thanks, too, to my very lovely husband, Markas, who provided
crisps, chocolate hobnobs, thesaurus and proofreading
services whenever needed, and who has really earned his
keep! Also to Sarah McHattie and Luisa Covill – you have been
splendid pals; and to anyone I have momentarily forgotten,
thank you, too.